# NEW JERSEY
## AND THE
# MEDAL OF HONOR

# NEW JERSEY
## AND THE
# MEDAL OF HONOR
## A HISTORY

### PETER ZABLOCKI

THE
History
PRESS

Published by The History Press
Charleston, SC
www.historypress.com

First published 2023

Manufactured in the United States

ISBN 9781467155304

Library of Congress Control Number: 2023938440

*Notice*: The information in this book is true and complete to the best of our knowledge. It is offered without guarantee on the part of the author or The History Press. The author and The History Press disclaim all liability in connection with the use of this book.

*For All the Veterans*
*Who Made the Ultimate Sacrifice,*
*And to Those Who Returned*
*And Remind Us that*
*Freedom Is Not*
*Free.*

# CONTENTS

# PREFACE

It was April 1862 when the men who would be forever immortalized as the "Andrew Raiders" failed to complete their mission, a fact that did not stop future historians from speaking of their feat in terms of legends. Nearly a year later, the last survivors of the failed raid to steal a Confederate train deep behind enemy lines (all while severely destroying depots, telegraph wires and train tracks during their return trek) assembled in a dark room with Secretary of War Edwin Stanton. Of the original twenty-five volunteers for the mission, eleven men had escaped or gone missing, the Confederacy hanged eight for "unlawful belligerency" and six were arrested as prisoners of war. These last men, recently released from captivity through a prisoner exchange, now stood in the claustrophobic space as the six-foot-tall President Lincoln entered the room.

A solemn but smiling Lincoln greeted the weak and malnourished men by telling them that American men and women would forever remember their actions. After shaking their hands, he exited the room through the same door he entered, only to return holding a small singular medal. The president then explained to the Union soldiers that Congress had recently approved the minting of a new award for valor. He then showed them a prototype of the medal that the six survivors of the daring raid would soon receive.

As the men stood in awe listening, Lincoln walked up to the only teenager and youngest of the group, Private Jacob Parrott. The president placed one hand on Parrott's shoulder and handed him the decoration with the other. This presentation inside the White House, without any fanfare, was the first-ever presentation of the Congressional Medal of Honor, the highest decoration for an act of bravery and sacrifice above and beyond the call of duty.[1] The date was March 25, 1863, and Lincoln could only hope that he would not have to hand out too many more, especially to the families of young men who were no longer alive to receive them, a sentiment undoubtedly felt by many of his successors in the years to come—and for most, a wish not granted.

# ACKNOWLEDGMENTS

As is always the case, this book would not have been possible without the constant support from my wife, Deidra, and words of encouragement from my sons, Lucas and Landon. I would like to thank Mr. Jack H. Jacobs for agreeing to read the first draft of the manuscript and provide support. I also wholeheartedly thank him for his service to our country. A sincere thank-you goes out to the people who were willing to read along and comment as I did my research and sent over chapters as I finished them, namely Steve Harding, Flint Whitlock and Steve Racine. Thank you to J. Banks Smither at The History Press for his support and for once again going along with another one of my research ideas. Also thank you to Mr. Brad Meltzer for words of encouragement as I was setting out to write these sometimes quite unbelievable stories.

# INTRODUCTION

warded by the president of the United States in the name of Congress, the Medal of Honor commemorates those who have shaped our nation's history and continue to inspire its future with their acts of valor, humanity, patriotism and sacrifice.[2] According to the official Medal of Honor Foundation, of the 40 million Americans who have served in the Armed Forces since the Civil War up to the present, only 3,515 have earned the Medal of Honor. Of that number, Congress has officially credited 93 honors to the state of New Jersey. While that number would be significantly larger if one only accounted for the recipient's birth state, this research aimed to examine only those medals accredited to the Garden State. The men whose stories grace these pages called New Jersey home when called up to serve their country and looked forward to the state as such when wishing to get back.

As the years progressed since Lincoln's first nonceremonial bestowment of the Medal of Honor on the young private Jacob Parrott in 1863, the U.S. Congress and the Medal of Honor Legion, founded in 1890, defined and redefined the requirements for receiving the nation's highest military citation. One of the first spelled-out stipulations concerned the point that the award be given for acts of distinguished service during battle or "in action involving actual conflict with an enemy."[3] Yet what clearly distinguished the American medal from those given in battle in other nations was the sheer fact that it did not require the men who received it to partake in a winning action that clearly benefited the United States. The

Medal of Honor was about individual valor and honor "at the risk of life above and beyond the call of duty."[4]

The only distinction to this last rule also pertains explicitly to the Garden State. Because the service on naval ships, especially around the turn of the twentieth century, was deemed dangerous, naval personnel could still receive the Medal of Honor during noncombat interim periods. Before 1945, when Congress forced uniformity between the different branches' requirements for the medal, one New Jersey man became the recipient of such a noncombatant medal when he jumped into stormy waters to save a fellow sailor. Ironically, Robert Augustus Sweeney did so not just once but twice—subsequently becoming one of nineteen double Medal of Honor recipients of all time and the only African American with that honor. An additional six New Jerseyans received Congress's highest citation during the interim period of the late nineteenth through the early twentieth century—all in similar circumstances of performing their "sailor's profession above the call of duty."[5]

Most Medals of Honor—more than 60 percent since World War II—have been awarded to men who never came home.[6] The men who lost their lives for their nation usually receive barely any mention in the annals of American history, apart from their stories being once covered in hometown newspapers. The latter stories became invaluable to this research.

Understandably, some of the stories have been lost due to the passage of time and scant recordkeeping detailing the specific acts of courage, as is the case with the thirty-five Civil War recipients from New Jersey. Others took place in conflicts long forgotten or little understood by the modern reader. Namely, these include partaking in the Boxer Rebellion in China in 1900, where three Garden State men had earned a Medal of Honor, or the Philippine Insurrection taking place simultaneously and resulting in two additional citations for New Jersey. Even more culturally sensitive by twenty-first-century standards are the Indian Wars that took place in the western plains of the United States following the Civil War. Five New Jersey men earned the nation's highest citation for their bravery against Native American warriors who were being forced onto reservations against their will. The same case can also be made for the six individuals from the Garden State who received their medals for actions during the short-lived and often-forgotten Spanish-American War of 1898, which saw the United States emerge as a global power.

The Civil War, the bloodiest military conflict in American history, also accounts for the most Medals of Honor awarded to troops in all three branches: the U.S. Army, the U.S. Marine Corps and the U.S. Navy. New Jersey follows the same general pattern where more than one-third of all medals awarded were granted during the 1860s conflict. Apart from some distinct stories of valor that have stood the test of time for one reason or another—as is the case with Charles F. Hopkins, who wrote down his still accessible memoirs—the majority of the stories are condensed to unremarkable citations. Of the thirty-five official accreditations, seven were given for capturing the enemy's flag, three more for leading a charge on an enemy encampment and another three for holding an enemy position once taken. Similarly ambiguous are citations of individual valor on naval ships, which vaguely state that the six New Jersey men, all on various ships, distinguished themselves in time of war. And while it would be possible to add to these stories, one could not avoid making too many generalizations that might detract from telling the men's individual accounts of bravery. As such, the book concentrates on the stories that best exemplify the United States' conflict of brother against brother without diminishing or diluting their counterparts' importance.

The records of honorable deeds got much better as the United States entered the First World War, which was also when Congress clarified and finalized the requirement for receiving the Medal of Honor—undoubtedly in anticipation of the American losses in the Great War. In the nineteen months that the American doughboys fought against the Central Powers, Congress would award 126 Medals of Honor to the soldiers, marines and sailors fighting for the Stars and Stripes—8 of which would go to men from the Garden State. By the time of the Second World War, which the United States entered in late 1941 after the Japanese attack on Pearl Harbor, that number more than doubled. In all, 473 Medals of Honor were awarded during the three years of fighting in Europe and the Pacific—this time with 16 going to New Jerseyans.

When it comes to the most talked-about and written-about conflict of the twentieth century, the Garden State is well represented. Nearly 560,000 men and women from New Jersey served overseas between 1941 and 1945.[7] The state's contribution is perhaps best highlighted through the fact that a New Jersey man was awarded a Congressional Medal of Honor in all the major theaters of the war—starting with zero hour at Pearl Harbor and followed by Africa, Europe and the Pacific. Even more remarkable is the varying nature of the acts that resulted in the nation's highest citation, with the precedent set on the very first day of American involvement on December 7, 1941. Forty-eight-year-old Peter Tomich, the chief watertender from New Jersey, serving on the USS *Utah*, sprang into action when it became evident that his ship would capsize from the two Japanese torpedoes that caused irreversible flooding to the hull.

That Sunday morning, the crew rushed to abandon ship as the USS *Utah* began to roll on its side just minutes after being struck at 8:00 a.m. Staying behind to man the fireroom to ensure that the boilers were secured so as not to cause an internal fire that would have undoubtedly resulted in additional deaths, Tomich allowed other engineers from the engine room to make it topside. The USS *Utah* rolled over at 8:12 a.m., taking 58 sailors' lives, including the man from New Jersey. For his contribution to saving the lives of 461 men, Peter Tomich was awarded the Congressional Medal of Honor—the first from his home state in the Second World War. He would be joined by eight of his Garden State brothers in making the ultimate sacrifice.

All of the stories in *New Jersey and the Medal of Honor* of men facing unbelievable odds read as if they come from comic books or Hollywood action movies and are often difficult to fathom while sitting in the comfort of our homes reading about them decades later. A case in point is the harrowing story of Private Nicholas Minue from Carteret, New Jersey, which closely resembles other heroic actions carried out by the men from the Garden State. Fighting with the 6th Armored Infantry, 1st Armored Division, near Medjez-El-Bab, Tunisia, during World War II, Minue sacrificed his life so that others in his company did not have to.

When the advance of his Company A was held up by flanking fire from an enemy machine gun post, cutting the men off from the remainder of the larger force, the Carteret man fixed his bayonet and charged the gun position "under a withering machine gun and rifle fire, killing approximately ten enemy machine gunners and riflemen."[8] Having destroyed the position, Minue continued his one-man charge into the German dugout positions, killing and routing more enemy soldiers until being fatally wounded by gunfire. His citation is quite simple, unlike others written about in greater detail and discussed in the following pages: "The courage, fearlessness, and aggressiveness displayed by Pvt. Minue in the face of inevitable death was necessary for advancing and driving the enemy from the entire sector."[9]

As the second "War to End All Wars" came to a close, it ushered in a new paradigm that saw the United States become the most powerful nation in the world—a status it fought to keep against its nemesis, the Communist- and totalitarian-ruled Soviet Union. And although the two nations never engaged in a full-fledged war against each other, the ideological conflict resulted in proxy wars, which would once more call on American men and women to sacrifice their lives to preserve their nation's ideals at home and abroad. On June 25, 1950, Communist North Korea, backed by Communist powerhouse China and the Soviet Union, crossed the 58th parallel of the Korean peninsula and attacked its southern neighbor. By the time of the armistice in July 1953, 191,000 New Jerseyans had served in the Korean War—4 would earn the nation's highest military decoration.

The conflict may have changed, but the sacrifice for one's nation was not much different from any other that came before it. Soldiers, sailors and marines once more placed the well-being of others before their own. Such was the case of First Lieutenant Samuel S. Coursen of Madison, New Jersey. The United Nations forces fought the Battle of Triangle Hill in October 1952 against the Chinese People's Volunteer Army to regain a forested ridge north of Gimhwa-eup—part of a mountain range that served as the central Chinese and North Korean concentration and communication area. During an October 12 engagement, heavy enemy fire pinned down Coursen and his company. As panic began to set in, some troops located a well-camouflaged emplacement thought to be abandoned and rushed for its cover. The New Jersey man held off just long enough to hear shots and screams coming from the bunker.

The former class president at Newark Academy, a football star and a graduate of West Point Academy might have thought of his high school sweetheart, now wife, and his six-month-old son back in Madison, New Jersey.[10] Yet Samuel was a natural leader—already twice decorated in the conflict, having received both the Bronze Star and the Silver Star for his heroism. If he wanted to return safely to his family, he needed to continue doing the right thing—and now that was rushing to the emplacement bunker to try and save one of his men. Coursen jumped into the unknown. He fired off a few shots from his M1 Garand, taking down a couple of enemy soldiers, and then used the stock of his rifle to battle the oncoming men. While his wounded comrade survived the battle, the Madison man did not. When his body was recovered after the battle, seven enemy dead were found in the emplacement, their heads crushed with Samuel's rifle.[11] True to one of the Congressional Medal of Honor's guiding principles, Lieutenant Coursen's citation was not awarded for victory in battle, but for individual action. As in many of the stories that follow, the military objective behind his actions was not always met. In Coursen's case, the mounting casualties forced the UN to abandon the hill to the Chinese after forty-two days of fighting.

New Jersey continued to be represented in arguably the most controversial proxy war of the Cold War if not all of American history. The Vietnam

War, fought with various levels of American involvement between 1955 and 1975, divided households, families and an entire nation. The conflict claimed the lives of 1,487 New Jersey soldiers—ordinary men drafted to fight in a war not many understood. For them, this war was not about politics, television commentaries back home or history books waiting to be written—it was about duty and survival. Three of the six men from the Garden State who received the Congressional Medal of Honor in Vietnam followed the lead of another New Jersey man who fought in Korea and never came home—they used their bodies as human shields. The stories of men jumping on grenades to protect their brothers in arms are not new to warfare or new to the men from New Jersey. And while one of the soldiers discussed in this book survived doing just that in World War II, the three who did attempt the same in Vietnam followed closer in line with Henry Svehla's actions in Korea.

Having already singlehandedly charged the enemy position in Pyongyang, Korea, on June 12, 1952, Private First Class Svehla was not quite done carrying out his heroic deeds. As if bullets spraying around him were not enough, a mortar round exploded near him, severely cutting his face. Even this did not stop him. His citation reads, "Despite his wounds, Private First Class Svehla refused medical treatment and continued to lead the attack. When an enemy grenade landed among his comrades, Private Svehla, without hesitation and undoubtedly aware of the extreme danger, threw himself upon the grenade."[12] The selfless action that cost the Essex County man his life was repeated by three more men from the Garden State in the Vietnam War.

Millions of Americans have entered the Armed Forces of the United States throughout history. Yet since the Medal of Honor's inception in 1863, only 3,525 have been awarded to American servicemen for acts of courage and selfless feats in battle. Setting out to tell the stories of New Jersey men who received the military's highest honor was a bit trickier than initially anticipated. As stated before, the first selection process eliminated those who were simply born in New Jersey and concentrated only on those who called the state home during their deployment or action. As such, men born in New Jersey but living in other states, like Edward C. Benfold, who appears as one of five Medal of Honor recipients on a plaque located at the New Jersey Korean War Memorial in Atlantic City, are not highlighted in the narrative. Even then, choosing which stories to tell and which to glance over was extremely difficult and often fell to how much available evidence existed to tell the entire story.

Each chapter of this book contains the narrative of one New Jersey man (or, in some cases, a few who acted together) and his action of heroism beyond the call of duty. It does so by placing their individual feats within the greater context of military history, thus helping us understand the impetus for the men finding themselves hundreds or thousands of miles away from their New Jersey homes. While undoubtedly heroic, the stories contained in *New Jersey and the Medal of Honor* do not set out to glorify war but rather to celebrate the men who answered their nation's call. Many books have been written attempting to understand why nations go to war, yet the intent here is not to seek that answer. Still, there is something to be said of President Herbert Hoover's 1944 quote: "Older men declare war. But it is the youth that must fight and die. And it is the youth who must inherit the tribulation, the sorrow, and the triumphs that are the aftermath of war."[13]

In "How to Tell a True War Story," from his award-winning Vietnam War novel *The Things They Carried*, author and Vietnam War veteran Tim O'Brien wrote, "In many cases a true war story cannot be believed. If you believe it, be skeptical. It is a question of credibility. Often the crazy stuff is true and the normal stuff isn't, because the normal stuff is necessary to make you believe the truly incredible craziness. In other cases, you can't even tell a true story. Sometimes it's just beyond telling." I set out with this message in mind. To tell the stories as they were remembered, written or spoken about. Sometimes even I found some of them unbelievable, which only added to my admiration for the men who played them out in real life. The book you now hold in your hands proves once again that sometimes the truth is scarier than fiction—in most cases, its frankness and honesty could not be any purer.

The bottom line is that the soldiers whose stories fill these pages fought and sometimes died for their nation and its ideals in the hopes that their sons and daughters would not have to do the same. I hope that this book will serve as a reminder to future generations that our nation's freedom—the things we take for granted, such as the ability to feel safe in our homes and to speak our mind—is not always free.

# PART I

# IN PEACE AND WAR, 1863–1916

*Make the world a better place by being more mindful of your children, thoughtful of the elderly, charitable to those less fortunate and open to opposing views.*

*—Leonard B. Keller, Medal of Honor recipient*

# THE 1ˢᵀ FROM NEW JERSEY

T he Battle of Gaines' Mill in the summer of 1862, part of Union general George B. McClellan's failed Peninsula Campaign to seize Richmond, pitted fifty-five thousand Confederates against Federal V Corps' thirty-five thousand, commanded by General Fitz-John Porter.[14] But for Union corporal Charles F. Hopkins and his men, it might as well have been a battle of David versus Goliath. The fighting had begun at 2:00 p.m. on July 27—a hot day by any measure. By 7:00 p.m., the fighting was all but over. Confederate forces had cut through Union lines in an all-out attack. For a moment, Hopkins, part of the 1ˢᵗ New Jersey Infantry, Company I, thought that his fellow troops would be spared from famed Confederate general Robert E. Lee's onslaught. But that was not to be.

For the men involved, this was not a battle but a descent into the pits of hell. Shells burst all around them, dropping sharp tree branches as the men retreated through the woods. "Our brigade was all cut to pieces, and some companies only had twenty men left," recalled one Union soldier.[15] The enemy deceivingly waved Union flags to disorient Porter's men while raising a black flag to show they would grant no mercy to those captured. "The rebels crushed our wounded soldiers in the head, knocking their brains in and running their bayonets through them."[16]

Just when it seemed they would remain in reserve, the 1ˢᵗ New Jersey, with Corporal Charles F. Hopkins's Company I, was ordered to cross the Chickahominy River to reinforce Porter's Corps. By then, most of the original Union forces had already been chased past it by Lee and his cavalry under the command of Thomas "Stonewall" Jackson. When it was time to leave the woods that night, half of the New Jersey force was killed, wounded, captured or missing in action.[17] Initially ordered to stand in reserve behind the artillery, the New Jersey men were hastily moved to the front of the line. The Confederates poured out of the woods, quickly overwhelming the reinforcements. Abram H. Paxton, first sergeant of Hopkins's company, yelled for the men around him to take cover behind the bales of hay set up earlier for breastworks and now bloodied from Porter's retreating troops. "We had not fought over half an hour before the rebels flanked us right and left… marching by as close as I ever saw," Paxton wrote. With the Confederates coming from seemingly every direction, Company I was surrounded.

Charles F. Hopkins, a skinny boy one month past his twentieth birthday, was far from his home in Hope, New Jersey. Having attended a one-room schoolhouse near what is now Ledgewood, the young man prided himself on his ability to read and write. Even during these trying hours, with projectiles, gunshots and death all around him, Hopkins probably checked his pocket for his small leather-bound diary. Regardless of his young age, the boy from New Jersey knew the significance of his role. Being raised by a successful businessman and a strong abolitionist, young Charles learned about the evils of slavery from a very young age. One might even say that apart from the Bible, he learned how to read from the abolitionist newspapers that his father made him and his five siblings read aloud after dinner.[18]

As he knelt behind a tree, surrounded by countless rebels, smoke and gunfire, Corporal Hopkins had to know that he could not stay hidden forever. He had been in plenty of scary situations in his young life, so this one most likely did not faze him. As a young teen, Charles's childhood home had become a station on the Underground Railroad, with his family regularly assisting people in their escape to freedom. As instructed by his stern father, young Hopkins spent many dark and dreary nights driving his silent passengers to the next station along their destination.[19] A few times, southern bounty hunters almost caught him, but the thought of failure prevented him from ever giving up.

It had been a year since Hopkins left his home against his mother's will— he did not say goodbye to his father for fear of being denied permission. Now he might never see him again. Perhaps Charles had thought about this since his early days in camp at Trenton. Even then, he had to know that the future ahead would not be easy, as he and his friends would spend most days foraging for food because the army did not allocate enough provisions to the 1st New Jersey. A lot had changed since those early days, when he first faced

Charles F. Hopkins, who died in Boonton on February 14, 1934, after waiting years for his award to be delivered due to a clerical error. *Congressional Medal of Honor Society.*

danger while away from home. Back in June 1861, an angry farmer fired his rifle at young Hopkins, who, along with one other, was eating the man's blackberries.[20] The scratched hands from their escape and the fruit-stained uniforms of that day, which looked as if the men had seen actual combat, would now be replaced with real blood and wounds that might never heal.

The fighting near the Chickahominy River was intensifying—if that was even possible. The Confederates were now fully encircling the Jersey regiments. The flanking brigade discharged its fire as the Union troops desperately attempted to make a stand—all for naught. "The order to retire while keeping up the fire, was given by our captain," Hopkins wrote in his diary. "Not hearing the order or unconscious of the dangerous position, the company did not retire promptly, and the enemy poured a terrific fire on us from every point but our immediate rear," he added. "And even that was not exempt until we reached a point parallel with the line of battle."[21]

Hopkins was on the move, musket fire splitting the air around him and tearing up the ground beneath his feet. The young New Jerseyan followed his orders—stop, reload, fire, turn around, run, stop. Soon it was evident that he was one of the few to do just that. The shot came fast and hard, and Hopkins dropped to the ground. Had he stayed, he would surely not make it out of the woods alive. The twenty-year-old soldier stood up and, keeping low, made his retreat, hearing voices all around him—the rebels were upon him, or he among them. Another shot, but this time Hopkins did not fall; he kept on going, twice wounded. "I was looking for shelter to cover by backward movement, and, while moving from one place to another among the bushes, came across Sergeant Richard Donnelly of our company."[22] Hopkins could not ignore the painful sounds coming from behind a thicket. It was getting dark by now, and it could have been anyone on the other side of the bush. Yet it was not in the New Jersey man's nature to ignore a plea for help.

Sergeant Donnelly's right leg was severely wounded—blood spilling out around the protruding bone. The younger soldier refused when the man told

Hopkins to leave him be. "I told him I would take him out of there, and we could both chance the awful fire from all quarters," he would later recall. Hopkins then lifted the wounded man on his shoulders. His legs buckled a bit, his wounds reminding him that sitting next to the injured Donnelly might have been a better idea. Hopkins moved rather slowly, grateful that the day was giving way to night. Then the yelling and firing of weapons in their direction dissipated any notions of not being seen. "I had [Donnelly] on my back and, through that gauntlet of flame and bullets, made my way to the rear in safety."[23]

Hopkins delivered the wounded sergeant to the first Union soldiers he encountered, unaware that one determined Confederate soldier never gave up the chase. When they heard the rifle discharge from the nearby trees, the few men who made up the last of the retreating Union line had barely finished putting the wounded Donnelly on the stretcher. The lone bullet hit the left side of Hopkins's head with enough force to knock him to the ground—like a marionette doll cut off from its strings. One of the Union men looked at the New Jerseyan's bloody face and signaled to move out before they, too, were killed. Having finally caught up with his prey, the Confederate soldier moved in closer to check on Hopkins's body. Undoubtedly, to his surprise, the young man, his face a bloody mess, was still breathing. In a twist of fate, the man put down his rifle and carried the Union soldier to a Confederate field hospital, where doctors removed one Minié ball and two buckshot from his head and neck. Barely conscious and able to walk, Hopkins was promptly released in the early hours of the next day along with other wounded men— the Confederates could not waste scarce resources on enemy prisoners.[24]

Within a few years, while fighting in Union general Ulysses S. Grant's 1864 Wilderness Campaign in Virginia, Charles F. Hopkins was captured and made a prisoner of war—he would spend the remainder of the conflict in the infamous Andersonville Confederate prison. After the war ended, Hopkins refused to talk about his experiences, instead hiding his fateful journal among inconspicuous things around his house. It was found by his grandson decades later and published in book form in 1988, and even then, it mentioned his heroic deed of carrying a wounded man out from behind enemy lines in only one short paragraph. The man who would later marry, move to Boonton, New Jersey and have seven children died in the Morris County town in 1934, but not before first becoming its mayor, a Morris County freeholder and a New Jersey state assemblyman.

Honorable to the end, Hopkins never applied for any recognition for his deeds. When the man whose life he saved that night heard that was the case, he recommended Charles for the Congressional Medal of Honor without the former one's knowledge. In a twist of fate, although awarded in 1892, due to a clerical error in the War Department, it was not delivered to Boonton, New Jersey, and Hopkins's hands until 1927. When the citation finally reached him, the former Union soldier was surprised to learn that he had carried Donnelly for more than one mile on his back while bleeding out from his two wounds. And even then, he thought it could not have been that long of a distance—after all, that would be impossible. But then again, it is often the impossible that makes the stories such as that of Charles F. Hopkins extraordinary.

As Charles F. Hopkins withered away at the Andersonville Prison in Georgia—death, scurvy and dysentery all around him—the war continued for his fellow New Jerseyans. Six hundred miles to the north, Sergeant James T. Clancy of Camden County took a deep breath, closed one eye and then exhaled. The bullet shot out with intent—thirty yards away, Confederate general John Dunovant would forever remain thirty-nine years old.

The Battle of Vaughan Road began on October 1, 1864, as part of the Siege of Petersburg. Starting in May, Union general Ulysses S. Grant threw everything at his Confederate counterpart in battle after battle—from Spotsylvania to Cold Harbor and finally to Petersburg, which remained under Union attack from June 1864 until 1865.[25] The actions were some of the most vicious of the entire war, seeing Grant lose as many as sixty thousand men within one month between May and June. The Petersburg Campaign, which aimed to cut away the city's four crucial supply railways from Richmond, was becoming less of a siege and more defined by raids, skirmishes and battles.

The October 1 attack on the Union army near the Vaughan Road, which included the 1st New Jersey Cavalry, lost its element of surprise when a Confederate brigadier general once dismissed from the United States Army for drunkenness, John Dunovant, accidentally rode into the American lines on the night of September 30. Having lost most of his scouting party to Union fire, the general insisted on clearing his name of the debacle by leading a frontal charge against American positions the next day. The action pitted him right against the 1st Cavalry of Maine, Massachusetts and New Jersey, whose orders were to hold their ground and, above all, not surrender any territory gained in or near Petersburg—no matter the cost.

The thirty-one-year-old New Jerseyan quietly observed the rain pelting the incoming Confederate lines. The fighting had started four hours before, at about 10:45 a.m., with the Maine Cavalry driving away the rebels' first assault. After trying and failing to gain ground against the Americans a second time, Confederate generals Wade Hampton and Matthew C. Butler suggested attacking the Union's weaker right flank. The plan that might have seen the Confederates drive the Union forces from the area was promptly overturned by an overly eager John Dunovant, who instead insisted on one other frontal assault—it would be his last.

Confederate brigadier general John Dunovant, who was shot by James T. Clancy. *Library of Congress.*

It probably did not take long for Sergeant James T. Clancy to pick out the tall man with a sword in his hand walking ahead of his troops. The officer was still far off, but the New Jerseyan continued tracking his movement. And then came the infamous rebel yell. Clancy lifted his rifle to his shoulder as the hordes of men charged at the well-defended dug-up Union positions.

Steady. Slow. The rain blurred his vision, but the target was too big to miss. The bullet struck Dunovant straight in the chest, ripping through his back and killing him before his lifeless body ever met the muddy ground beneath his feet.[26] Farther in the back of the advance, General Hampton yelled for one of his medics to rush toward the fallen brigadier general, only to see a bullet cut him down as soon as he got near the body. Without an officer to lead them, the Confederate lines ran aimlessly as the Union forces cut them down, one by one.

Clancy continued reloading his weapon and firing, yet none of the other shots he made that day was as important as his first. Dunovant's brigade faltered and retreated within minutes of its leader's death, suffering 130 casualties in mere moments.[27] The commotion caused by the failed frontal assault led the Confederate generals to forgo further engagements for the rest of the day, granting the Union forces enough time to build up its weaker right flank. While some attributed the shot that turned the battle around and allowed the Union troops to continue their siege of Petersburg to Clancy, a shot that would ultimately result in the war's victory, others were not so sure. Still, enough evidence and testimonies, including Clancy's, corroborated the story to make the New Jersey regiment commander, Major Myron Beaumont, recommend him for the Congressional Medal of Honor. President Andrew Johnson awarded him his medal on July 3, 1865—one of thirty-five Medals of Honor accredited to the state of New Jersey.

# THE FORGOTTEN FEW

The man's rank did not faze him—an "ordinary seaman," stated the paperwork, the lowest naval rank. Yet Robert Augustus Sweeney could probably care less. The short African American man stood topside and listened to the creaking of the wooden-hulled gunboat, the USS *Yantic*—only twenty years old and already a relic of the Civil War. The 179-foot ship stood still in New York Harbor, having just returned from a relief expedition in Greenland in preparation for a tour of South America and the West Indies.

The other sailors moved like ghosts around seaman Sweeney, not noticing him. Just another African American cook, steward or landsman— none ever higher in rank than a third-class petty officer.[28] The New York winter of 1883 was relatively mild compared to the historic blizzard that would dump fifty-eight inches of snow on the state just five years later. But Sweeney could still feel the December breeze hit his face as he scanned the surrounding docks. Set up in 1801, the Brooklyn Navy Yard was the nation's most famous shipbuilding facility. It garnered its fame for the construction of the USS *Monitor*, the first ironclad warship commissioned by the U.S. Navy, a feat it would soon follow with the 1889 launch of USS *Maine*, the first modern battleship.

Seaman Sweeney had no reason to look away from his white brothers in arms. Especially since, unlike the shy young man avoiding their stares, the rest of the USS *Yantic* crew had not been awarded the highest military decoration. The USS *Yantic* was not Robert Augustus Sweeney's first tour of duty, nor was it his first ship. The young man began his navy career just two years prior on the USS *Kearsarge*, a single-gun deck Mohican Class Civil War ship. When the *Kearsarge*, with Sweeney on board, docked in New York in May 1883, the boat's storied career was all but over. Robert transitioned to the USS *Yantic*, while USS *Kearsarge* stayed in the Brooklyn Navy Yard in preparation for its last tour before eventual decommissioning.

The USS *Yantic* might have been his new home, but Sweeny still looked at the empty nearby dock from where the USS *Kearsarge* departed for its final

The USS *Yantic*, from which Robert A. Sweeney jumped overboard to save a fellow sailor's life and earn his second Medal of Honor. *Library of Congress.*

voyage just a few months prior. For a brief moment, the sailor's mind might have wandered back to the *Kearsarge*.

The weather in Virginia on October 26, 1881, was nothing like New York now. The winds that day made the flags dance more than they were willing to, and even the current December wind could not match forces with the storm assaulting Virginia's Hampton Roads harbor two years before. The wind and the high tide welting the ship's portside almost masked the scream—or was it the rain hitting his face that made him hear things? The twenty-eight-year-old African American ran toward the rail and looked down below. It was dark, and the rain made it difficult to tell where the ship ended and the water began. The sailor was drowning, struggling for air—and then, just as quickly as Sweeney noticed him, the man was gone, swallowed by the angry water.

It had been two years since that day—yet, as if in a trance, in his mind, Robert was still back in Virginia on board the USS *Kearsarge*. The young sailor remembered everyone shifting portside and yelling for the drowning man. And then he remembered hitting the water. It tore him in every direction, swallowing him like the sailor he was instinctively trying to save. Sweeney dived and searched for his shipmate while struggling to come up for air. And then he got him. Robert grabbed the younger sailor by the collar and dragged him to the shore with all his might. It did not matter that the young man was white and that Sweeney was Black. The United States would fail to acknowledge their equality for another sixty years until President Harry S Truman's Executive Order 9981 finally desegregated the Armed Forces in 1948. But in 1881, in the Virginia waters whose clutches Sweeney was desperately trying to escape, race equality was still an unattainable dream, even though that day showed that death would not discriminate based on skin color.

Robert Augustus did not tell his new shipmates of the heroic deed, nor did he tell them about the Congressional Medal of Honor he received and promptly sent back to his family in New Jersey. None of that mattered. On the USS *Yantic*, he was once more just another Black man among many, a seemingly invisible sailor.

Standing there in the December breeze two years later, Sweeney probably vividly remembered his life-defining event. Based on the record of that day, we can assume that he knew that if given a chance, he would do it again, even in the turbulent racial times of post–Civil War America. To the low-ranking Sweeney, any life was a life worth saving. And then it happened: the scream, a splash, then another and then a cry for help.

Sweeney was already running across the deck toward the nearby moored USS *Jamestown*, another soon-to-be decommissioned Civil War–era single-gun deck ship. This time, somebody was already in the water trying to save the drowning man. In fact, as Sweeny had done two years before, the twenty-one-year-old British immigrant J.W. Norris wasted no time jumping after his fellow seaman when he fell overboard. But now, instead of helping, he too was being dragged down by the panicky A.A. George, who had just fallen in.

Looking on from the deck of the USS *Yantic*, Sweeney undoubtedly thought of the coldness of the water during the winter months. He was born in the West Indies but spent most of his time living in New Jersey, across the harbor, and knew the Northeast winter. The men could not survive in this water for too long. The recipient of the Congressional Medal of Honor— one of the few African Americans to be granted the honor—did not need to think anymore. Sweeney's body hit the water with urgency. He was right; the New York harbor was much colder than the Virginia waters two years ago.

Robert Augustus Sweeney, the only African American to have earned the Medal of Honor twice. *Congressional Medal of Honor Society.*

30

Robert Augustus Sweeney's USS *Yantic* would leave the Brooklyn Navy Yard for South American waters in early 1884, this time with the only African American to win two Congressional Medals of Honor onboard—both for saving a life of a man overboard. At the time, unfortunately, Sweeney was still just another Black man with the lowest possible rank in the U.S. Navy.

Within four years of Sweeney's departure from New York, the shipyard's Building Way One lay a keel for a new class battleship. The USS *Maine*, which the navy finally launched in 1895, mysteriously exploded in Havana Harbor in 1898, contributing to the United States' entrance into the Spanish-American War—a conflict in which two other African American boys from New Jersey, who were mere children during Sweeney's exploits, would distinguish themselves by acts of valor beyond the call of duty.

At the start of the Spanish-American War in 1898, about 2,500 of the nation's 25,000-man army were experienced African American soldiers.[29] By the time it ended, there were 13,000 Black men in the military, with four regular and one volunteer regiments, partaking in the fight against the Spanish empire. While President William McKinley was initially hesitant to allow African Americans to volunteer or serve in the new war, outside pressure from Black leaders and organizations pushed him to incorporate the established units into the expeditionary force. Due to the oppression and racism in the United States, these Black troops felt empathy toward the Cubans and thought that the Spanish injustices perpetrated against the locals needed to end. Similarly, many African Americans were motivated by the belief that honorable military service could speed up the arrival of equality and dignity back home.[30]

Americans watched the Cuban War of Independence against the brutal Spanish forces under Governor General Valeriano Weyler from the onset of the Cuban revolution, yet it was not until the explosion of the American battleship USS *Maine*, stationed in Havana Harbor, that the United States decided to act on their reservations against Spanish rule in the Western Hemisphere. After watching his demand of having Spain grant Cuba its independence ignored in April 1898, President McKinley asked Congress for authority to intervene "to stop the misery and death, protect American lives and property in Cuba, curtail damage to commerce, and end the onerous task of enforcing neutrality."[31]

American troops landed in Cuba on June 22, 1898, just three short months after a mutual declaration of war between the nations of the United

States and Spain. The initial force numbered seventeen thousand men, including four Black regiments: the 9th and the 10th Cavalries and the 24th and 25th Infantries. Out of the four regiments, the 10th Cavalry was the most distinguished. One of the original "Buffalo Soldier" units created after the Civil War, the regiment made a name for itself through its participation in General William T. Sherman's winter campaigns of 1867 and 1868 against western natives and their gallant fighting in the subsequent Indian Wars. Now, the 10th was the first all-Black unit utilized when the Americans engaged the Spanish at Las Guasimas just two days after landing in Cuba. The African Americans' actions that day led one member of the more famed 1st Cavalry Regiment, the "Rough Riders," to proclaim, "If it hadn't been for the black cavalry, the Rough Riders would have been exterminated."[32]

Within a week, the 10th would once again be involved, this time in a special operation to reinforce and land supplies to Cuban revolutionaries on the Tallabocoa River near the town of Tunas de Zaza. By the day's end, two African American men from New Jersey would earn the Congressional Medal of Honor.

Privates George Henry Wanton (thirty) and William H. Thompkins (twenty-six) were far away from their hometown of Paterson, New Jersey. The task now at hand seemed onerous. Yet the two men and a few of their brothers in arms from the 10th Cavalry never expected anything different. The American steamships *Fanita* and *Florida* left Key West for Cuba five days earlier, protected by the gunboat USS *Peoria*. On board the ships, besides provisions, thousands of guns and horses meant to aid Cuban insurgents, were 350 Cubans under General Emilio Nunez, 50 troops of the 10th United States Cavalry and 25 Rough Riders.[33] A sudden Spanish military buildup near the mouth of the San Juan River made the simple task of disembarking the troops and supplies nearly impossible from the first day the ships arrived on June 29, 1898.

After reaching another potential drop-off place higher up the river on the evening of June 29, the three American boats disembarked a small scouting party in a rowboat to pull to shore, only for the men to be assaulted with rifle fire coming from an abandoned blockhouse near the shoreline. The captain of the USS *Peoria* deemed the area unsafe and continued sailing farther eastward. The next day, the three ships reached the area of Las Tunas near the mouth of the Tallabocoa River. Staring at them from the shore was a large fort built of railroad iron surrounded by earthworks.[34] After firing several shots at the fort without a response, the captain sent another scouting party to shore. This one was much larger and consisted of fifteen volunteers under the commander of the Rough Riders, Winthrop Chanler, and another fifteen Cubans under Captain Nunez.

A moment after the boats reached the shore, about five hundred yards from the fort, the large structure came alive with a barrage of gunfire. Captain Nunez fell instantly from a bullet to the head, while another round tore through Chanler's arm. The Americans and Cubans ran into the thickets for cover, only to watch the Spaniards set their sights on their boats, which they quickly rendered useless. While

Private George Wanton, who aided in the rescue of his wounded comrades during the Spanish-American War. *Congressional Medal of Honor Society.*

the *Peoria* shelled the fort with volley after volley, some of the members of the scouting party tried swimming back to their ships, only for the Spanish bullets to cut them down before they could make the effort count. Only one would break through, naked and scraped from fending off sharks and bullets. As the last remnants of the sun hid behind the USS *Peoria*, the handful of stranded survivors, seeing no other hope, retreated away from the fort and deeper into the brush.

It was nearly midnight when Wanton and Thompkins and two additional Buffalo Soldiers, Dennis Bell and Fitz Lee, sat quietly in their wooden rowboat—their paddles gently cutting through the still water so as not to make too much noise. Only an occasional shark fin broke the stillness around them. Above the four men of the 10th United States Cavalry was nothing but a dark sky illuminated by the sea of stars. It was June 30, 1898, their date with destiny. After three failed attempts to send a rescue party to collect the stranded men near the fort, theirs was the latest—this time under complete darkness. Implied was their selection based on their skin complexion, yet nobody would admit it, not even their commanding officer, Lieutenant Ahern, who sat in the back of the boat with a low hat covering his white face.

Shortly before setting off on their rescue mission, the men of the 10th Cavalry got some reprieve after USS *Peoria*'s guns cut off the advancing Spaniards' position to the east of the fort from the perceived location of

William Thompkins of Paterson participated in the raid to locate American survivors of an attack gone wrong in Cuba in 1898. *Congressional Medal of Honor Society.*

the American and Cuban survivors. At the moment, apart from the crickets, toads and other animals of the night, all seemed silent. The four men reached the half-sunken boats of the original scouting party and, as slowly and as quietly as they could, jumped into the water and hid behind the splintered wooded structures. Ahern remained with the boat, while the four men moved forward.

The first of the many bodies Wanton and Thompkins saw was that of Captain Jose Nunez, brother of General Emilio Nunez, the Cuban politician and the face of the island nation's independence movement. As the men scanned the shoreline using only the moonlight as their guide, the four New Jerseyans could not find the man they were primarily sent to retrieve, the Rough Rider Chanler.

About twenty yards past the shallow beach, the land gave way to a mangrove swamp and forest. The trees and their long roots sticking out of the mudded water looked like caricatures from an Edgar Rice Burroughs novel. The men saw no other choice but to move into the waist-deep muck to continue their search. A few single volleys came from the fort's direction—undoubtedly a trigger-happy sentry dissuading the Americans from sending yet another scouting party. Thompkins stopped in his tracks and signaled for others to do the same. Luckily, the firing stopped. Their biggest enemy now was the swamp, which continued to swallow them up the deeper into the woods they went. The animal noises around them grew louder as the trees severely hindered their already poor visibility with their high and exposed roots. The mosquitos attacked their faces and necks as the men continued—losing hope with each step toward the dark unknown.

It was nothing short of a miracle that Thompkins, Wanton, Bell and Lee found the survivors. In fact, had they not made the trek, the stranded men would surely not have lived through the night. The three men who survived were found submerged to their necks in the swampy waters, their faces dirty and bloody. Held above their shoulders was the floating body of the gravely wounded Chanler, who could no longer stand without drowning. The boys from the 10th Cavalry had found what they were looking for, and not a moment too soon. After making an equally perilous journey back to their boat with the wounded man and the two survivors, the African American soldiers realized that dawn was upon them—a fact not missed by their Spanish counterparts hiding in the fort. Without further delay, and this time with bullets flying above them and tearing into the water around them, the men rowed back to the American ships with all their might.

Another rescue mission would leave early that day and locate five more survivors, primarily Cuban—this one not led by any member of the 10th Cavalry. The USS *Peoria* was now assisted by a larger gunboat, the USS *Helena*, which arrived that morning with further reinforcements, which were promptly let off farther down the shore for the land assault on the Spanish fortification. With the barrage of fire coming from the two gunboats and the Cuban and American troops having finally landed to support the attack, the Spaniards stood no chance. The fort fell on July 3, 1898.

By the time the four Buffalo Soldiers received their Congressional Medals of Honor for their daring rescue mission nearly one year later on June 30, 1899, the war with Spain was long over, and the United States, having beaten an empire, was now a world power. Yet while the nation's status in the world changed, the same courtesy was not extended to all the men who fought to make it happen. Many more African Americans would have to give their lives for their nation before it was ready to see them all as most of their brothers in arms already saw them—as equals.

# CABLE RAID OF CIENFUEGOS

T he small wooden cabin situated thirty feet from the shore looked innocent, yet on May 11, 1898, it was the place marker for a dangerous American voyage into the Spanish-controlled harbor of Cienfuegos. Seamen Robert Blume and Hudson Van Etten's boat left the *Nashville* battleship at half past six o'clock in the morning. The men, allowed to dress any way they desired, except not in white so as not to provide an easy target for the Spaniards, wore scant clothing—even at such an early hour, the weather was already unbearably hot. The sailing boats—one leaving from *Nashville* and one just like it launching from the *Marblehead* with another New Jerseyan onboard, George Frederick Mager—were recently modified for the task at hand. Each boat consisted of a crew of sixteen, of which twelve were rowers such as the three Jersey men, Blume, Van Etten and Mager; there was also one coxswain, one officer, a carpenter's mate and a blacksmith.[35] The decision to take the small number of men was based on the high likelihood of considerable casualties and thus limiting the inevitable deaths by only committing enough individuals needed for the task.

The two steam cutters, armed with machine guns and artillery and commanded by selected Marine Corps sharpshooters from their respective battleships, towed the two boats to within three hundred feet offshore before throwing off their launches. The three men from Jersey and their brothers in arms picked up their oars and began rowing closer to shore. Next to each man lay a rifle for the inevitable fight that would soon ensue. Strapped to their hips were revolvers on the off chance that their boats got stranded close to shore and they would need to fend off the Spaniards at close quarters.

Yet the real weapons for this unique mission lay piled together in the middle of the wooden boats. These were tools for finding and cutting underwater cables, namely cold chisels, blacksmiths' hammers, a heavy maul, a block of hardwood with an iron plate for its upper surface, an axe, wire cutting pliers, a hacksaw and coils of stout rope and grapnels of different sizes.[36] And while the Spanish army prepared for an invasion by marching 1,500 men to nearby Punta de la Colorados, the thirty-odd sailors with two small gunboats and two battleships in reserve had no intention of attacking the shore. Their raid was much more complicated than that.

BEFORE THE INVENTION OF radio and internet, the number one means of communication between the war front and military headquarters, or even between a colony and its subjugating nation, was through telegraphic cables. To prevent the constant cutting of wires by local Cuban revolutionaries, the Spanish government devised a plan to hide a string of telegraph cables underwater near the coast. Encased in a lead and iron tube, the main communication lifeline of the Spanish empire in Cuba, which connected not only the nation within itself but also the entire colony with the outside world, proved to be the perfect deterrent for locals who lacked the means to find and disrupt it. Through local intelligence, the American navy learned of a small shack near Cienfuegos that served as the main link between two main wires, one heading northwest toward Havana and one east to the Cuban port of Santiago and then to Jamaica and to the outside world.[37]

On May 1, 1898, the Department of the Navy tasked Commander Bowman McCalla and, in turn, Lieutenant Cameron Winslow with leading a raid on the structure containing the telegraph hub and machinery. Yet even more important was locating the two cables, leaving the structure whose permanent damage would be much harder to repair than the small building. After much deliberation and preparation, Winslow was ready for his raid.

The two battleships *Nashville* and *Marblehead* entered the narrow opening of Cienfuegos Harbor in the evening hours of May 10, 1898. The naval force approached the harbor through a three-mile-long channel. The men first noticed a large lighthouse erected about twenty-five yards from the shore. The telegraph cable structure was directly in front of it and only about twenty feet from the water. Between the two buildings lay a system of rifle pits concealed by tall grass and bushes. Large coral formations that broke the approaching sea waves extended along the shoreline and in front of the two structures—making landfall nearly impossible. That would be just fine

The gunboats approach the shore during the Cable Raid of Cienfuegos. *From the* Century Quarterly *(March 1899).*

for Lieutenant Winslow; the battleships' gun barrage could take care of the telegram building. It was the cables, which had to be somewhere near it, that he and his crew wanted. The only thing to do now was to find them, raise them from the bottom of the harbor and sever them. These were the simple directions given to Blume, Van Etten, Mager and their counterparts before they entered their rowboats. Within minutes of departing their respective battleships and being dropped off near the shore by their supporting steam gunboats, the men realized that carrying out the orders was far from simple.

Some Spanish troops were in plain sight as the boats approached the shore, but the same could not be said for the larger force or the cannons hidden in the trenches. The reefs and corals drew nearer, clearly visible through the white foam created by the crashing waves. And then the *Nashville* and *Marblehead* opened up, projectiles flying low above their heads in search of the telegraph house. "Again and again, the shells found their mark," Winslow recalled later. "[They were] bursting and sending clouds of stone and mortar into the air, demolishing wall after wall, until one shot, striking the tottering structure, burst and brought it down, leaving nothing but a disordered pile of masonry covering the wreck of electrical instruments."[38] The marines in the gunboats behind the men tasked with finding the cable also opened fire, drowning the hastily started Spanish counterattack.

Blume, Van Etten, Mager and the others were now in a crossfire, a fiery hailstorm of bullets around them. The boats needed to get closer, so the oars were manned, and in a column, the men rowed closer and slower to land, where the water was shallow enough to identify the cable on its bottom. When the bullets tore into the sides of the rowboats, the sailors took out their cartridges and, instead of loading their rifles, used the shells to plug in the holes in their wooden hulls. "As the boats neared the shore, the anxiety due to anticipated fire from the enemy increased. The launches were only a few lengths apart, and every man in the boats was exposed and plainly visible,"

Winslow wrote in his report.[39] The process of finding the cables began when the boats were finally within one hundred feet of the shoreline, with the small gunboats covering fire from about fifty feet behind them.

With the dark patches of coral giving way to the white sand underneath them, the men could see 30 feet below them and promptly threw the grapnels overboard—the dragging to find the cables had begun. Only when the hooks began getting caught in the reef did the men decide that they needed to get even closer to shore, where the water was less than 20 feet deep. Dodging bullets, it was George F. Mager's boat that found the first cable. The man from New Jersey and *Marblehead* launch's crew labored to lift the heavy object from the bottom of the harbor, which they then hooked with additional ropes under it and worked over to one corner of the stern of the boat. After lifting the cable over the second boat, the two vessels separated to conduct their cutting of what would eventually amount to about 150 feet of the heavily reinforced cable.

On the *Nashville* launch, the crew, which included Blume and Van Etten, used axes and chisels, only to find out that their small handsaws, about nine inches in length, would do the trick. The men labored below the incoming and outgoing rifle and cannon fire, all while changing hands with the one handsaw they brought per each boat. After about thirty minutes, both boats successfully cut the cable and set off to look out for the second one.

To the dismay of the men on the boats, their search brought them closer and closer to the Spanish volleys—and it was not until they were nearly upon them that the second cable was discovered. "We were directly in front of the rifle pits and hardly a hundred feet from them. The ships, realizing the danger of our position, increased their fire until it became a furious cannonade, the shells passing so close over our heads that the crews instinctively ducked as they went by and burst against the rocks beyond."[40] The men then proceeded to repeat the feat. "We realized that we had to take the chance of an accidental hit from our ships or receive the enemy's fire at pistol range, and the men worked on in disregard of both."[41]

The second cable proved more stubborn than the first, a matter made only worse by the now-concentrated Spanish fire coming from the lighthouse. The commanding officer yelled for the men to hurry up, for any more time spent would surely mean death. At one point, the frazzled Winslow even went about grabbing the hacksaw himself while at the same time directing the small gunboats behind him to fire past and at the Spanish positions. As if on cue, the sailors finally managed to cut off one hundred feet of the cable. Winslow saw another line a few feet away, much smaller. But before he could order

Robert Blume was one of three New Jersey men to earn the Medal of Honor for his contribution to the Cable Raid of Cienfuegos. *Congressional Medal of Honor Society.*

his men to throw down their grappling hooks, the Spaniards opened up with much-renewed ferocity. Bullets whizzed past the men, who no longer dared to stand upright in their boats.

George Mager looked toward the gunboat covering their retreat just in time to see a marine fall overboard as a bullet ripped into his face. Within seconds, another man, this one right next to the man from New Jersey, dropped to the bottom of a boat with a similar wound. About ten yards away, in the *Nashville* dingy, Blume and Van Etten were undoubtedly sprayed with blood as the head of one of their counterparts seemingly exploded from a nearby shot—a wound later described as having left a six-inch gap in the man's skull.[42] The sailors, not engaged in firing their rifles, began rowing back toward the battleships—their mission accomplished. All left to do now was to survive to tell the tale.

The launches made it past the small gunboats fairly quickly. And even though their craft was now shielded from the Spanish bullets, the men continued rowing with all their might, as if their lives depended on it. By the time the gunboats reached them to begin hauling them to the *Nashville* and *Marblehead*, the rowboats were already more than halfway to them. The sailors and their marine counterparts were under fire for nearly three hours. Amazingly, only two men died, one from each service branch, with others suffering severe injuries.

Notwithstanding the odds against them, the American raid was successful in severing two ocean cables, which cut off the Spanish communication on the island and hastened the end of the war. The cutting of the cables connecting Cuba to the rest of the world in May 1898 resulted in fifty-two men receiving the Congressional Medal of Honor. The most undoubtedly harrowing moments of George F. Mager, Robert Blume and Hudson Van Etten's lives would be immortalized in just one sentence: "During the cutting of the cable leading from Cienfuegos, Cuba, May 11, 1898, and facing the heavy fire of the enemy, [Blume, Mager and Van Etten] set an example of extraordinary bravery and coolness throughout this action." A simplified narrative of what happened, but then again, sometimes, no matter how much one tries to convey the real story, it can never match the intensity of the truth.

# PART II

## THE GREAT WAR

*We enjoy today because of those who came before.*
*We will leave the country better than we found it for those who come tomorrow.*

*—Robert E. Bush, Medal of Honor recipient*

# MAKING THE WORLD SAFE FOR DEMOCRACY

The Meuse-Argonne offensive, the last Allied push against Germany that would see the Great War come to an end, had turned the forests of France into an inferno of destruction. Historians would later refer to the September to November 1918 engagement as America's bloodiest operation; the soldiers of the 78th Infantry Division called it for what it was: hell on earth.

The New Jersey 78th Division was activated at Fort Dix on August 23, 1917. Within a few short months, its young men would find themselves part of the United States' biggest offensive since the American Civil War of the previous century. Soon the French would change the explanation for the origins of the division's insignia, a lightning bolt on a red background. What was once a tribute to "white lightning" moonshine distilled near its training camp became a homage to the 78th Division's fighting style, resembling a bolt of lightning that left the field blood red.[43]

William Sawelson was with the 312th Infantry of the 78th Division since it left Hoboken, New Jersey, on May 12, 1918, for ports in England and then to Calais, France. The twenty-three-year-old man from Harrison, New Jersey, was initially sent to the front with the British for four-day tours before being transferred along with the entire 78th into the American sector and the U.S. 1st Army under General John Pershing on August 10, 1918.

The 1st Army spent the next month fighting in a joint-French operation near St. Mihiel, a German bulge on the western line near the province of Lorraine characterized by thick forests and winding creeks. The terrain was miserable as the men from New Jersey witnessed their first carnage of the kind of battle that Europeans called reality for the past three years. One soldier later recalled enemy artillery fire falling night and day with deadly accuracy. It racked the nerves of men with "the continual sight of dead and wounded." The rain fell persistently, "with only occasional hours of brilliant sunshine; clothing was rotting with mud and water; and guns and equipment could not be cleaned owing to the failure of the supply of gun oil."[44]

The first week of October saw the men of the 78th Division move to assist in clearing the Germans from the area between the Meuse River and the Argonne Forest and penetrating Germany's main defenses, collectively known as the Hindenburg Line. Arriving a few

William Sawelson crawled through heavy machine gun fire to aid a fallen soldier. A German bullet cut his life short. *Congressional Medal of Honor Society.*

weeks into the Argonne offensive, which began on September 26, Sawelson's 78th Infantry Division was ordered to relieve the 77th Division near the town of Grand Pre. The objective to secure the town and its surrounding woods was made more difficult by the well-fortified German positions and the fact that both Grande Pre and the Bois des Loges woods held high ground in the surrounding area.

The men attacked with supporting artillery firing above them from behind. Like the rest of the war, characterized by stalemates and trench warfare, the fighting often resulted in hand-to-hand combat and little gains. And while the New Jerseyans were able to make some ground in securing Grand Pre, the surrounding woods were proving to be impregnable. From October 20 to October 23, Sawelson and his comrades fought to exhaustion. "One of the American groups would often work their way well into German lines and then, finding that it was alone, would have to fight its way back again," recalled one soldier.[45]

The resistance was heavy, and the machine gun nests were seemingly everywhere as William Sawelson's battalion found itself pinned down beneath a hill in yet another attempt to gain ground at the Bois de Loges. It was Wednesday, October 23, 1918, and the Harrison, New Jersey man had only moments to live. The men found cover wherever they could as fire rained down on them from every direction but up—and even that was questionable, as bullets kicked up muddy divots around them. As most of the

Historians would later refer to the Meuse-Argonne offensive as America's bloodiest World War I operation. *Library of Congress.*

men found a ditch or a fallen tree to hide behind, the battalion's commander ordered all men to stay put—this after a failed attempt to get a runner out. Private Parker C. Dunn would receive a Medal of Honor for his effort to do just that before being cut down by a German bullet.

The men waited, encircled by heavy smoke and fog. Trees, or what was left of them after being cut down by machine gun fire, burned from previous artillery attacks—a familiar smell of a bonfire mixed with death and destruction. It almost seemed peaceful—almost. One could hear the occasional burst of gunfire, a cry from a nearby shell hole or a not-so-silent prayer. William Sawelson heard it all, but then he picked out the faint call for help. Moving from his position would surely mean death, but what would staying and doing nothing mean? Swanson, crawling out of his hiding position, moved slowly toward the pleading man. When he reached his brother in arms, he knew that he could not do much more than comfort him and give the man some water. After the wounded man drank the remainder of what was left in William's canteen, he pleaded for more. When Sawelson turned to leave, the man grabbed him and made him promise he would return. William nodded and began crawling back to his shell hole.

After securing additional water from another fallen man's canteen, Sawelson set back to keep his word. The machine gun burst came quick and loud, breaking the Jersey man's promise. The Meuse-Argonne had claimed another member of the 78th Division—one more of the total of 4,989 by the time the offensive ended.[46] The man from Hudson County, New Jersey, would remain in the Argonne forest forever: Plot C, Row 9, Grave 33, Meuse-Argonne American Cemetery—a Medal of Honor symbol carved into his white stone cross.

Within two days of Sawelson's death on October 23, 1918, the city of Grand Pre finally fell into U.S. hands. The Germans retreated back and regrouped east of the city, only for the 78th to give chase. By the time the men from the Garden State made it into position for another battle, the Germans had left. It would be the end of the war for Sawelson's fellow soldiers. Had he lived another week, the Medal of Honor recipient from New Jersey would have been able to tell his story to his family personally—instead, they had to read about it in *Camden Post-Telegram*'s April 24, 1919 edition.

JOHN OTTO SIEGEL WAS German by birth, which was quite a predicament at a time when the United States was in an all-out war against Kaiser Wilhelm II's nation. Due to his previous court-martial for desertion, the twenty-six-year-old Newark, New Jersey resident was already under a watchful eye. The scrutiny only made his work on the U.S. naval tugboat *Mohawk* in the Norfolk Naval Shipyard that much more difficult. He undoubtedly longed to see his wife and young daughter back in the Garden State, the woman for whom he ran away from the navy to marry in 1915, only to be confined to hard labor for a whole year as a result.[47] But that was before the Great War—before Woodrow Wilson broke his promise of keeping "us" out of it.

It was November 1, 1918, and nobody knew that the war would end in ten days, especially not Boatswain's Mate Second Class John O. Siegel. The Norfolk Naval Shipyard around him looked the part of the oldest and largest industrial facility in the United States. Everywhere he looked, men were at work repairing, modifying or constructing new sea vessels—with a vigor and urgency that had not ceased since America entered World War I in April 1917.

One could not miss the flames if they tried. The schooner *Hjeltenaes* was one massive fireball just seconds after Siegel spotted the first inkling of a fire. The New Jerseyan jumped off his docked tugboat and raced across the pier. It was not that the men around him were too slow to react and come to the boat's aid; it was just Siegel's urgency that made him look like a sprinter among walkers. The German American disappeared into the smoke and flame as others raised the alarm and made way for fire rescue crews and hoses. Siegel emerged from the fire carrying one man only to go right back into the blazing schooner. He would rescue one more man before returning to the flames one last time. The smoke made him feel dizzy, and his hand had to shield his eyes from the excruciating heat as the sailor entered the crew's quarters. It was empty. As Siegel turned around to leave, a steam pipe ripped open directly above the exit door, trapping him inside. And then darkness.

Seeing the daring man enter the burning *Hjeltenaes* on multiple occasions, Siegel's shipmates finally decided to follow the sailor's lead when he did not emerge. It was the rescuer that was now the victim. After carrying him out and rendering first aid, the New Jersey man regained his pulse but not consciousness. Local papers reported that "Siegel was in such condition that a medical officer worked over him most of the night, and for a while, his life was despaired of."[48] John survived and returned to work at a receiving ship for another year before again deserting the navy for three months.

During his 1920 court-martial, it was revealed that at the time of his action on the *Hjeltenaes*, the German American was severely depressed. The strain of service away from home and discrimination toward his nationality had taken a toll on his marriage.[49] Suddenly the lives of others were more important than his own. Not putting too much stock in receiving the Medal of Honor, Siegel would lose it, ironically, in another fire while employed as an ironworker in the 1930s.


IT WAS THE DAWN of October 3, 1918, and Private Frank J. Bart of Newark, New Jersey, was about to partake in what historians would call the "most skillfully executed American divisional attack of World War I."[50] For Bart, it was just another day that put him closer to the end of the war and his home in Essex County.

Although Frank enlisted in Newark and should have been assigned to the New Jersey 78th Infantry Division, he became one of the hundreds of men used to plug up new and depleting divisions. Assembled from spare units in late October 1917, Bart's 2nd Division was the only one of Major General John Pershing's original four to be organized in France instead of the United States.[51] In all, Private Frank J. Bart would go on to serve with Company C, 9th Infantry Regiment, for twenty-three months. By the time he returned to the Garden State, his decorations included the Medal of Honor, two Silver Stars and the Purple Heart from the United States; the Medaille Militaire and three Croix de Guerre from France; the Italian Medal of Honor; and the Montenegran War Cross, as well as the New Jersey Distinguished Service Medal.[52]

When Bart passed away in Lyndhurst in March 1961 at eighty-five, no one would have suspected that the elderly bachelor was among the most decorated New Jerseyans of all time. Bart only ever spoke about his experiences at his American Legion Hoboken post with other members of the World War I generation—and even then sporadically.[53] For the forty years he was a Legion member, the veteran watched as old age claimed his fellow soldiers one by one.

Frank J. Bart ran ahead of his line in World War I France, silencing numerous German machine guns and protecting his fellow soldiers. *Congressional Medal of Honor Society.*

By the time his nephew took him in to care for him two months before his death, there was not anyone left to listen, even if he had wanted to recall his heroic deeds from forty years before.

As William Sawelson trekked through the Ardennes with the 78th Division in an assault on the German Hindenburg Line, his fellow New Jerseyan Frank J. Bart's 2nd Division provided the necessary cover. The all-but-forgotten battle of the Blanc Mont Ridge, which would see Private Bart earn the Congressional Medal of Honor, began on October 3, 1918. The German defenses on Blanc Mont Ridge stopped the French 4th Army from securing the necessary cover for the American advance into the Meuse-Argonne sector. The French commanders then asked Pershing to loan additional troops to break the deadlock, lest he be left with an open left flank.[54] The American general sent in the 2nd Division and, with it, the thirty-five-year-old Newark man, Frank J. Bart.

The assault plan to take the ridge was different from prior infantry maneuvers, as it called for a gradual and phased battle that would see two brigades lead short forward advances, wait for the artillery to move up before continuing upward and then repeat the process until the hill was taken. In their way stood countless machine gun nests, dug-out trenches full of Germans, mortar positions and heavy artillery.

In his memoir, marine John Thomason recalled the day when he, Private Bart and hundreds of Americans advanced up the ridge against impossible odds. The gray and misty dawn had been quiet up to that point when, at 5:50 a.m., the French and American heavy guns opened up with one tremendous crash. The New Jersey man watched as the ground in front of him "was swept by a hurricane of shellfire; red and green flames breaking in orderly rows where the 75s showered down on the [German] lines—great black clouds leaping up where the larger shells fell roaring."[55] It was time to advance up the hillside, its woods veiled in low-hanging smoke.

The fierce machine gun fire cut into Bart's Company C as it made its way up, forcing the men to use cut-down trees and whatever they could find for cover. The group of men, getting smaller with each yard gained, found an empty German artillery dugout. The respite was brief, as the order was given to continue before any of them could take advantage of the relatively safe position. "It was unsafe to stand upright, as quite often some machine gunner turned the muzzle of his machine and raked our [temporary hiding place]," a soldier recalled.[56] The boys of the 2nd Division crawled when they had to, anything that would get them to German trenches, where they could take a temporary break if they were lucky. In fact, "If it had not been for the trenches that ran along the crest of the ridge, I do not believe we could have held our gains."[57]

Just as Company C cleared another crest of a rise, fierce machine gun and artillery fire pinned the men down with no means of moving forward. The artillery was relentless as it zeroed in on their position—staying in place meant sure death, as did any movement toward the well-concealed machine gun nest. Only Frank J. Bart knew what came over him that moment. The New Jersey man was used to running; after all, he was the company runner. Frank grabbed one of the few new M1918 Browning automatic rifles—issued to some men the month prior—from a nearby soldier. Unlike the heavy machine guns with large ammunition boxes, the Browning's twenty-round box magazine and a sling belt holster made this new invention a deadly mobile weapon.

Bart sprinted between trees as if in an obstacle race—veering left and then right. The bullets ripped into the woods around him. When near the machine gun nest, the private made a quick turn, running past it. Before the Germans inside could turn their fire, Private Bart and his newly acquired Browning automatic rifle had already flanked them. Frank was likely still out of breath when his brothers in arms moved up to meet him as he stood among a handful of dead German soldiers. There was no time for congratulatory handshakes, as the day was just beginning for Company C, 9th Infantry, 2nd Division. The men continued up the ridge, albeit slowly and with many casualties. Forced into hand-to-hand combat on a few occasions, the 2$^{nd}$ Division's plan of securing ground and waiting for support and artillery to move up was working to perfection.

By the day's end, Private Frank J. Bart would repeat his feat, once again running toward assured death with his borrowed M1918 rifle. One can only assume that after single-handedly silencing another machine gun nest, nobody in his company dared to suggest that the Browning rifle belonged to anyone but him. Although it took a few days, the 2$^{nd}$ Division secured the ridge and held it against strong counterattacks for the next few days, sustaining 4,821 casualties.[58]

Private Bart's actions of October 3, 1918, which would gain him the Congressional Medal of Honor, came right between the war's two most famous events resulting in the same citation. The day before, on October 2, Major Charles W. Whittlesey's battalion of mixed troops from different companies of the 77$^{th}$ Division found itself cut off and surrounded behind enemy lines in the attack on the Meuse-Argonne region. As Bart ran ahead of his line and silenced machine gun nests, Whittlesey and his men held on against all odds until they were finally rescued on October 7. Of the 670 men of the "Lost Battalion," only 191 would survive to tell the story.[59] Like Private Bart and Major Whittlesey, Corporal Alvin York's deeds that same week would earn him the Medal of Honor. On October 8, the one-time conscientious objector from Tennessee, part of the 82$^{nd}$ Division, led his own private war against a German position, firing into enemy lines and single-handedly securing 135 prisoners.

Frank would live to see his two fellow Medal of Honor recipients' stories immortalized in popular culture—with the latter even receiving a major Hollywood blockbuster treatment starring Gary Cooper in the title role. Private Bart probably did not mind. Like the other two men depicted on the screen and in literature, he was not in it for the glory. He was just another young man trying to do anything to hasten the war's end and return home.

# THE JERSEY BOYS OF LE CATELET

**W**ars and battles are often examined through statistics; the biggest this, the longest that or the first ever. Yet to the men on the ground, none of it matters; they do not see the main objective apart from their specific order or task. And at the end of the day, only one statistic matters: their own life.

The battle began at early dawn on September 29, 1918, moments before thousands of men and hundreds of tanks set forth against the German-held sector of the Hindenburg Line near the St. Quentin Canal on the outskirts of the northern French town of La Catelet. The New Jersey men Sergeants Alan Louis Eggers and John S. Latham and Corporal Thomas E. O'Shea of the 107th Infantry, 27th Division, attached to the 4th French Army, watched anxiously as 1,600 Allied heavy guns fired nearly 1 million shells at the German positions in the span of thirty minutes—the greatest British artillery bombardment of the entire Great War.[60] The twenty-nine-year-old Rutherford, New Jersey man, John S. Latham, would recall the day that immortalized his bravery in a letter to a friend back home. "Jack, the stunt we pulled off on the 29th was a hell-hole, and no mistake about it. We tackled the toughest part of the Hindenburg line and smashed it, too, and in such a way that the Germans saw the beginning of the end when that drive commenced."[61]

French marshal Ferdinand Foch perhaps correctly called the attack the "greatest of all battles." Eight Allied armies were about to converge on the weakening Germans—the Americans and the French 4th Army from the east, the British 1st and 3rd slightly more centrally, with Belgians and British groups in support, and the 4th British and 1st French from the west. The main objective was to concentrate on securing the German position near the St. Quentin Canal, south of Vendhuile, where it ran underground for six thousand yards through the Bellicourt Tunnel—now converted into a critical German defensive position on the Hindenburg Line.[62] The canal was the only location on the infamous defensive line separating the two fronts where the Allied tanks could cross the Escaut River. Securing it was imperative to the overall success of the entire operation.

The three New Jersey men with the 107th Infantry were about to partake in the largest coordinated offensive of the Great War, one whose purpose was to show the German kaiser that the war was all but lost.[63] Yet by nightfall of Sunday, September 29, 1918, in northern France, the 107th Infantry would suffer the greatest number of casualties sustained in a single day by any U.S. regiment in the great conflict.[64] By the day's end, only two of the three New Jersey friends would make it back home alive.

It was 5:30 a.m. when Latham, Eggers and O'Shea's 107th Infantry, 27th Division, began the main offensive across "a battlefield enveloped by autumn mists and low-hanging clouds."[65] The advance of the American 30th and 27th Divisions' was spearheaded by the freshly trained 301st Heavy Tank Battalion and the war's newest invention, British Mark V tanks. The goal was to secure the Le Catelet–Nauroy defensive line east of the St. Quentin Canal to cover the leading British and French thrust toward the canal and tunnel. The men, each with a rifle in

Alan L. Eggers (*top*), John S. Latham (*middle*) and Thomas E. O'Shea (*bottom*). *Congressional Medal of Honor Society.*

hand, crept silently through the fog while taking shelter behind the forty thunderous tanks rolling forward unopposed. The closer they got to the

German trenches and fortifications, the more difficult it became to breathe, which was undoubtedly the result of the thirty thousand mustard gas shells deployed in the initial barrage. Still, had it not been for the high explosives sent along with it, the line would have been difficult to cross due to the miles of barbed wire, which now lay tangled and ripped apart for Americans to get across.

The initial success of the 301st Heavy Tank Battalion proved to be the infantry's undoing. While the machines quickly pushed beyond the Hindenburg Line, they left behind many unseen and uncaptured strong points along the line that opened fire at the incoming troops. The 30th Infantry found itself among unrelenting machine gun fire, causing mass confusion and isolated combat. The German gun positions were everywhere and connected by underground passages unseen by the American troops, who desperately sought any possible shelter in the infamous no man's land separating the enemy trench system from Allied lines. The close-range machine gun fire engulfing the units made it impossible for individual troops to advance.

It was into this hell that the three men from New Jersey set off with the 27th Division across the wide-open expanse of land pocketed with shell holes, mud and dead bodies. It was soon evident that the preceding British artillery fire that supported the American attack came down beyond the powerful German positions on the knoll and farmland past the Le Catelet–Nauroy defensive line. The missed defensive position now opened withering machine gun fire and artillery on the 27th Division.[66] Together with the other seventeen men of the 3rd Platoon of the 107th Infantry, Latham, Eggers and O'Shea dodged a hailstorm of fire.

First to go were the tanks, which fell victim to German artillery and mines and became nothing but places of cover. But even those soon became unsafe, as they attracted the attention of the seemingly endless fire of machine gun nests that troops preceding the 3rd Platoon passed by in the fog. "Most of the divisional zone between the jump-off point and the [German line] became one vast maelstrom of violence," a soldier later wrote.[67] Latham, Eggers and O'Shea were now right in the center of it. The men of the 3rd Platoon ran for cover, with the smoke barrage coming down directly on top of them. As was often the case, the three Garden State men kept close to one another, and when Latham and Eggers found a nearby shell hole, they dragged O'Shea down along with them into it. The men buried their faces in the dirt and covered their helmets with their hands, waiting for some respite. Eggers might have thought back to a happier time when he was a student at Cornell

American units advancing on the Hindenburg Line. *Library of Congress.*

University, a place he left to enlist in the U.S. Army and one the sergeant likely now wished he could return to when the war was over. But first he and his two friends needed to survive this day.

The mud encased the men's uniforms, water seeping into their shoes. Getting out of the crater was out of the question, yet staying far from guaranteed survival. Latham, Eggers and O'Shea listened to the dying sounds of battle, distant machine gun bursts and screams moving farther down past the German lines. They were alone—encircled by countless German outposts.

It is amazing what one can hear in silence after a battle has moved on—the creaking, smoldering machinery with random artillery pops, the slowly fading sounds of death and, above all, the stillness. In a letter to his wife, an American soldier once wrote of his time during the Great War, "It is remarkable how the birds still sing in the war-swept [fields]."[68] They did not know how long they lay there, the mud on their faces now hardened. At first, they could only distinguish the low German chatter in the distance—to their relief, never getting too close for comfort. There was a time they heard someone running, then gunshots, followed by more silence. And then came the cry for help. Initially quiet and then a little more pronounced. "Help."

One of the men slid up the crater wall, his body and face so close to the muddy surface that he was almost part of it. Looking out was a risk, but if the person calling for help did not stop, the Germans were bound to hear it and come searching. About thirty yards from the shell hole stood a British Mark V tank, a large hole blown up in its side. The fog made it difficult to see, yet Latham caught some movement from within the twisted metal. He lowered himself back down and informed Eggers and O'Shea of their predicament. They could stay where they were and hope that whoever was in that tank did not bring down a German patrol on them, or they could leave and try to save the person in need of help. Either option seemed equally wrong and right. After some consultation, the Jersey boys decided to attempt the rescue, especially as whoever was in the tank continued his cries for help.

They moved slowly in a staggered formation a few feet apart, keeping their bodies low to the ground. The nearby sound of the launched mortar gave it away before anything actually hit them. "Run!" one of them cried out as a slew of six hundred rounds per minute erupted from well-concealed MG-08 heavy German machine guns. The bullets pelting the ground around them were relentless. The men, "assailed now by a fury of small-arms fire, narrowed their eyes and inclined their bodies forward, like men in heavy rain, and went on [toward the tank]."[69] Eggers did not hear the shot nor see his best friend thrown to the ground. O'Shea was there one moment and then gone the next. They were nearly there, the wounded man inside the crippled machine now covering the two men that were left with fire from

An Allied tank like the one the Jersey boys used as a defensive position, destroyed by a German mine in the attack on the Hindenburg Line. *Library of Congress.*

his rifle. Latham and Eggers slid into the giant hole left by a mine in the tank's sidewall. Eggers noticed that his friend from Summit, New Jersey, was not with them and attempted to run back into the crossfire when Latham pulled him back into the tank. Instead, the men watched as bullets made the ground dance around O'Shea. Bleeding from a stomach wound, the Jersey man was about halfway between the tank and their original position. He was still breathing, yet going out to get him now would have been suicide, so the two men and the wounded officer of the 301st Heavy Tank Battalion, who they came to rescue, waited.

The stillness of half an hour ago was now broken by machine guns and rifles, populating the air with wicked keening noises.[70] The men continued to shield themselves inside the tank's twisted remnants. Eggers reassured himself by watching O'Shea crawl into a low ditch—perhaps his friend would live to see the day. It was now that they could see the carnage around them, bodies of men cut down as if wheat stalks on a field. The realization that their current position could only withstand so much, especially as it made a perfect target on an otherwise plain landscape, made the men think of a way out. When O'Shea disappeared behind the mound he was lying behind just a moment ago, the stranded men saw that it was not a ditch at all that their fallen brother had found but rather a makeshift sap trench.

Latham and Eggers waited for the machine gun fire to calm down, but the tank's exposed position continued to attract the swarm of bullets ricocheting off its shell. While one lifted the wounded officer on his shoulders, the other soldier fed the five-round magazine into his 1903 Springfield rifle and pulled back the bolt, sliding a round into place. It was time to go.

The distance to O'Shea's position seemed longer than it really was, even though getting there seemed to go faster than it should have taken them. The German guns, perhaps not anticipating the move, were slow to open fire and accurately take aim. As the Americans moved, one worked the bolt-action rifle and the other ran ahead, holding the wounded man. History lost the account of who did the firing and who the carrying, but it did not misplace the story of how the two Jersey boys managed to make it into the trench and reunite with their fallen friend. O'Shea was in worse shape than they thought, and although still breathing, he had lost consciousness. This new position provided the men with the much-needed cover, but if they were to hold it, they would need more than their rifles. They knew just the place that could get them their machine gun. The problem lay in the fact that it was back in the broken tank, and it would take some wrangling to detach it from its mount. But that was only one of the problems; first they had to get back to the tank. Would the Germans think them stupid enough to try to repeat the stunt they just miraculously pulled off?

It is amazing how ordinary people do extraordinary things in difficult situations, especially when reading the Medal of Honor citation given to the three Jersey Boys of Le Catelet. Not wasting the moment of surprise, Latham and Eggers left their wounded men behind and, staying low, "ran in the face of violent fire" back toward the tank.[71] Using their trench knives and tools found inside the wreck, the men detached the heavy Hotchkiss machine gun and collected all the feed strip ammunition boxes they could carry. For the third time that day, Latham and Eggers ran for their lives. Not wanting to be hit—and likely amazed by the fact that they had not yet been hit that day—the runners jumped into their trench head first. By then the Germans had had enough. Within moments, the enemy sent out the first patrol to kill the four Americans who continued eluding them. Latham and Eggers took care of this first patrol using their Springfield rifles and pistols. They would hold off the next dozen or so that followed throughout the day using their newly acquired tank machine gun.

By the evening hours, the Germans, perhaps having lost enough men trying to kill the pesky Yanks, took a break, and once more the battlefield was silent and still. When the sky was dark enough to cover their movement, Latham and Eggers grabbed the wounded men, with the tank officer having since also lost consciousness, and set back toward the Allied lines using the stars as the guide. "As always…the far horizon [behind them] glowed with fires of war—flares, signal lights, and gun flashes from hidden batteries."[72] Yet the men did not look back but continued silently—until they heard the right words in the correct language, "Who goes there?"

The American divisions were relieved early the next day, September 30, 1918, with some remnants of the 27th continuing the attack with the Australians until October 1. By the end of the first day, which saw Latham, Eggers and O'Shea stuck behind enemy lines, their 107th Regiment had 337 men killed and 658 wounded.[73] Yet as far as statistics go, the overall assault met its objective at the St. Quentin Canal, resulting in the first breach in the heretofore impenetrable Hindenburg Line.

Sergeants John C. Latham and Alan Eggers and Corporal Thomas O'Shea of the army were presented with the Congressional Medal of Honor on December 11, 1919. It was the only time during the Great War that three medals were given for the same action.[74] Unfortunately, Latham and Eggers had to watch as their friend Thomas O'Shea's award was accepted by his family on his behalf. While the officer they rescued went on to recover, the twenty-three-year-old O'Shea did not live longer than a few moments after the three Jersey boys made it out of no man's land. He was buried with other members of the 107th Regiment at the nearby Somme Cemetery in Bony Aisne, France, where he remains to this day.

Keeping a promise he made to himself when hiding in the shell hole that September day, John Latham returned to Cornell for law school after the war and went on to work on Wall Street until 1959.[75] He died at eighty-seven in 1975 and was buried at Arlington National Cemetery near his dear friend Alan Eggers, who had passed away a few years before. The three Jersey Boys of Le Catelet were together again.

# AN IMMIGRANT'S JOURNEY

The six-foot-tall, forty-five-year-old Eric A. Dime, the owner of the American News Service and the New York representative of the *Philadelphia Journal of Commerce*, sat down in his impeccable suit opposite the shy little Dutch American. The respected journalist had recently watched from the steps of the state capitol building as New Jersey governor Edward I. Edwards presented the young Sergeant Louis M. Van Iersel from Glen Rock, Bergen County, with a new medal.[76] It had been two years since the end of the Great War, and the five-foot-five immigrant was one of the bravest and most decorated men of the American Expeditionary Forces. In fact, since Dime requested this interview a few days earlier, the twenty-six-year-old Van Iersel was notified that the Medaille Militaire, the highest military honor conferred by the French government, had been added to his decorations.

The famed journalist could not pass on one of the most curious stories of the Great War—that of a small, shy Dutchman's transformation from a munition worker in Germany at the start of the conflict into a hero of the American army by its end. The two men met in Louis's home in Bergen County, his first ever home in the United States and where the famed New Jerseyan agreed to tell his story—one of the few times he would do so throughout his life. At twenty-six, with the boyish shy smile and slight build, Van Iersel appeared more like a teenager than a grown man about to recall the horrors of war. The article "How the Shy Little Dutch Sergeant Won that Dazzling Array of Medals" would run in all major newspapers across the United States and form the basis of Van Iersel's famed narrative.[77] After sitting at what might have been the kitchen table, Dime took out his pencil and notebook and scribbled the date on the top, April 1920. "Why don't we start at the beginning?"

THE KRUPP GUN WORKS in Essen was one of Germany's most famous gun makers. When the war began in July 1914, the great complex worked around the clock to produce the heavy artillery and siege guns the kaiser's army would use to subvert all of Europe. The young Dutch's journey to grim heat and intense war production at the German plant began in Dussen, Holland, five years before. With the sea at his doorstep and no prospects of a good life, the sixteen-year-old Louis set off on a life of a sailor. Sailing on the German river Rhine taught him to speak German, a language he picked up quickly at a young age. When the war started draining Germany's human resources, the nation appealed to foreigners to fill out its war production jobs. And while getting into Germany's workforce was relatively easy for Louis in May 1916, getting out just seven months later would be a much bigger challenge. Working for the Central Powers of Germany, Austria-Hungary and the Ottoman empire did not seem right for the young Dutchman. Yet men were too precious of a commodity in Germany for him to leave unopposed.

Sneaking into the nearest port, Van Iersel discovered a Dutch sailor and begged him to hide him past German patrols on the ship's journey to England. After days of hiding in the ship's bilge tank, Louis made it to England and resumed sailing on the *Little Secret*, a British freighter running between Liverpool and New York. It was in this capacity that war first touched the young man. While out to sea near Newfoundland, Van Iersel's freighter found itself battered by a vicious storm. As if trying to keep their boat afloat were not tricky enough, the *Little Secret*'s crew came upon small lifeboats thrashed about in crazy zig-zags by the sea. Inside the wooden boats were what was left of the crew of a Danish vessel, the *Olaf Marks*, which had just been torpedoed by a German submarine.[78]

Unwilling to leave the men to die, Van Iersel and one other crewmember lowered their own lifeboat into the treacherous waters and paddled toward the stranded men. Both the Life Saving Benevolent Association of New York and the British government would later award the young Louis medals for his feat of saving the lives of five casualties of Germany's unrestricted submarine warfare. When docking in New York in 1917 with $1.53 to his name, the Dutchman had no identity papers, which brought him to a recruitment office that allowed him to file for American citizenship,

Louis M. Van Iersel transformed from a munition worker in Germany at the start of the conflict into a hero of the U.S. Army by its end. *Congressional Medal of Honor Society.*

concurrently enlisting him in the U.S. Army.[79] Louis Van Iersel became Private Van Iersel, no. 40857, U.S.A., a member of Company M of the 9th Infantry of the 2nd Division, and was one of the first fifty thousand to leave America for the war with France.[80] He was on his way to fight for a country where he did not yet have a home—although he would make one in New Jersey right after returning—in a war that had already claimed millions of human lives.

Louis recalled learning to speak English very quickly, the third language he now communicated in fluently, thus integrating himself hastily into his Company M. It also did not take long for the young man to receive his first medals—a Croix de Guerre and a Silver Star—at the battle of Soissons. The engagement was part of the Aisne-Marne counter-offensive to the German Spring Offensive in March 1918, where the kaiser's army tried to defeat the Allies before the American entrance into the war. Sitting in his kitchen in 1920, Louis recalled to the journalist eagerly taking notes how early in the engagement he had been wounded in the right hand and arm and forced to get back to a field hospital, only to be back at the firing line within an hour.[81] The army had a hard time getting all the wounded away from the front lines, and Van Iersel volunteered to help, his shot-up arm and all—he was wounded twice more in the process.

Eric A. Dime must have looked perturbed by the matter-of-factness in Van Iersel's voice while he recalled the story; still, the humble hero continued. During the last stage of the same battle in late July 1918, Louis's battery was driving back the Germans, only to be stopped by a single machine gun nest, manned by one man. "This fellow had a good position; he was getting an alarming number of Americans with his sweeping shower bullets."[82] Van Iersel lay on his stomach in a shell hole that was not quite big enough for him and exposed his feet. Then the bullets from the machine gun blew away the soles of his shoes. "I was darn sore about [them]," the sergeant leaned in and said to Dime. "I made up my mind I'd get that Hun! When you're sore like that, you forget bullets." The Dutch American ran over toward the

Mine craters on Combres Hill near the Battle of St. Mihiel. *Library of Congress.*

machine gun, jumped into the hole, smashed the German's head with the butt of his rifle and took his shoes. "I counted sixty-seven bullet holes in my breeches when I got back, yet only a few minor scratches!" The so-called scrapes might have been more than Louis alluded to, as while his exploits allowed his company to advance, he wound up in a military hospital for the next five weeks.

When released back into his unit, Louis Van Iersel and the 2nd Division were ordered to partake in the Battle of Saint-Mihiel. Until the Normandy invasion in the Second World War, Americans knew September 12, 1918—the start of the attack on Saint-Mihiel, a major Allied victory, and the first United States–led offensive of the war—as "D-Day." During the bloody battle that lasted five days, Van Iersel added a palm to his Croix de Guerre when, together with two men, he held back a whole German battalion until American reinforcements arrived. Only three of the fifty-nine men who took the defensive position in the shell hole survived.

The Dutchman chuckled when the journalist stopped writing and inquired about the other palms on Van Iersel's Croix de Guerre. "It was a practical joke," said Louis.[83] Put in charge of seven men and ordered to investigate the enemy positions for about one thousand yards ahead of the American troops, Van Iersel made it about halfway when he told his men to stay back as he moved forward. "Suddenly, I found myself amid an enemy machine gun nest, so I bellowed out in German for them to come out." To his surprise, a frightened German officer blew his whistle, and there was a rush of men from the nearby dugouts. "The poor men thought themselves surrounded!" The small sergeant returned to the American lines with five German officers and sixty men—all his prisoners.

THE INCIDENT THAT GRANTED Sergeant Louis Van Iersel his most crowning decoration took place on November 9, 1918, only two days before the signing of the armistice that ended the war. The bridge in the town of Mouzon was supposed to have been blown away by the Germans. Yet there it stood, twisted and blackened by smoke but still spanning across the Meuse. Per previous reconnaissance reports, the enemy position across the river numbered about fifteen men, making it safe for the 9th Infantry to cross. Still, the captain had a feeling.

"The captain called me in and asked me if I would go on another scouting mission," Van Iersel recalled in a later interview. He was used to being the one chosen and did not mind. "It was because I spoke so many languages." The officer ordered Louis to act as reconnaissance for the battalion by crossing the bridge and reporting on the entrenched German positions. As he was allowed to take five men with him, the odds of successfully making it across were very high, especially if the enemy numbered barely over a dozen. The sergeant wasted no time assembling his group. "The ones I picked out went through a lot—they were good boys. You need someone you could depend on for an action like that."[84]

"I remember it was dark and cold as hell when we set off toward the bridge," Iersel later recalled.[85] Once they got to the structure's base, the men realized that calling the bridge intact would have been a lie. In fact, apart from the main support structure, most of the track going across was below in the water, in heaps and piles of debris. The men proceeded cautiously and acrobatically across the bridge's frame until about halfway through when, suddenly, machine gun fire rained on them from the other side. Two of his men fell dead instantly, while the rest of Louis's patrol scattered to hide behind the damaged portions of the once sturdy structure. Within a few short moments, stray bullets struck two other members of the party. A panicked soldier, seemingly the only one who came out unscathed, ran back across the bridge to tell the commander that none of the party had survived the crossing.

When the guns opened up, Van Iersel wasted no time hitting the deck. Yet instead of crawling back to the Allied side of the river, the sergeant continued inching closer toward the Germans. Suddenly the wooden plank he was over gave way, plunging Louis one hundred feet down into the Meuse. "The star shells from the German side made the bridge as bright as day."[86] Clinging on to a piece of wood, Van Iersel fought against the current for 150 feet to make it to the opposite bank. Having made it this far, the young man decided to complete the mission and gather the needed intelligence on the enemy positions. He climbed up the steep, muddy embankment, staying as close to the ground as possible. "It was so dark, and I couldn't really see, so I had to climb higher, and then all of a sudden, the Germans started shooting," Van Iersel remembered. "Jesus, boy, they opened up with everything they had." Louis buried his face in the mud and continued moving farther down the embankment and away from the bridge.

The guns continued until they deemed no one could have survived the barrage. Meanwhile, Van Iersel, this time more carefully, continued back up and along the top of the edge, gathering information. To his surprise, the supposed 15 or so men rumored to guard the bridgehead were more like 150, including seven well-hidden and secured machine gun nests on each side of the bridge. It would later become known that, in reality, more than 1,200 Germans occupied the town, and had the commander not sent out a scouting party, the American 9th Infantry would have walked into mayhem. Sitting along the enemy line, Van Iersel could not know that, but he did know that the situation was worse than expected and that he needed to let his commanding officer know.

Carefully, to avoid making too much noise, Louis went back down to the river and began swimming to the other side. When he made it, he realized that there was no natural way for him to make it up the rocky embankment, so he began climbing the bridge's vertical structure. "It was very slippery, and I was barely halfway up when the Germans shot up a flare, lighting up the sky again."[87] As bullets sailed toward his position, Van Iersel's dirty figure, now clenching for his dear life to the post, was indistinguishable from the rest of the structure. The flare stayed up for about one minute until it finally died out and the Germans gave up the chase. Van Iersel had made it—and in the process saved hundreds if not thousands of Americans about to cross the river. The order was postponed until a barrage of artillery hit the town and reinforcements arrived to help cross the Meuse.

IT WAS IN MARCH 1919, during the 2nd Division review in a town in Germany, when General Pershing presented the shy young man with the Medal of Honor for his actions on that bridge back in France. Right before the ceremony began, Iersel walked around nervously on the stage, passing various generals and men of higher rank than him, also about to be recognized in some form, when Lieutenant General John A. Lejeune stopped him. "Are you lost, Sergeant?" he asked. "No sir," the shy soldier answered, "I am here to receive a medal." The general looked the small man up and down.

"Ohh yeah, what kind?" Van Iersel looked up, embarrassed. "I believe the Congressional Medal of Honor, sir." Lejeune laughed and patted the young man on his back. "Son, you can stand any damn place you like to stand!"[88]

A few months later, at the Inter-Allied Games, a multi-sport event held in June 1919 at the newly constructed Pershing Stadium in Paris, France, Van Iersel found himself facing the king of Montenegro, reviewing the American troops and athletes. The king stopped in admiration before the extensively ribboned breast of the short man and, in bewilderment, asked American general John Pershing, walking with him, who this hero was. The American officer did not lose a beat, having remembered Van Iersel and thus quickly recounting his story. The king reached into his pocket and took out another medal, adding it to the already vast array on Louis's chest.[89]

At the time of Eric Dime's interview, Van Iersel had settled in Glen Rock, New Jersey, where he soon opened up a small general store in nearby Passaic. The journalist finished his interview and thanked the humble man, who walked him to the door. Without all his medals, Louis Van Iersel looked like just another young man full of life and hope for a better future. No one would have suspected that this short and gentle-looking man, speaking with an accent and who had only received his American citizenship months before, was one of America's biggest World War I heroes. Even Eric Dime could not quite wrap his head around the story he now had to go home and type—something he would readily admit.

# PART III

# WORLD WAR II

*When something needs to be done, push ahead and overcome all obstacles—there is always a way.*

—*Jay Zeamer Jr., Medal of Honor recipient*

# THE ISLAND OF DEATH

On Monday, February 19, 1945, the American forces hit the beaches of Iwo Jima island, 750 miles off the coast of Japan, fast and hard. The island's three airfields were indispensable to the planned invasion of Japan—a fact known to the Americans as well as the twenty-one thousand Japanese defenders entrenched in Iwo's volcanic Mount Suribachi.

John "Manila" Basilone of Raritan, New Jersey, led his platoon off its assigned amphibious landing craft tank 3C27 onto the infamous black sand beach of Iwo Jima. The twenty-seven-year-old looked the part of a heroic soldier—always standing tall, regardless of the dangers around him. Above John, the machine gun section leader on Red Beach II, and his men stood the fearsome fortress. Mount Suribachi dominated the island's skyline and overlooked the landing beaches and the southern ground leading to the airfields.[90] The former was the primary objective Basilone and other men of the 1st Marine Division, 7th Marines, 1st Battalion, set off to secure.

Their boots hit the black sand, sinking just enough to hinder any swift movement. The drudgery was all around them—no tropical climate so often attributed to South Pacific Islands and no foliage, just a cold, craggy, barren volcanic island.[91] Manila Jack, as he was known to his friends, ordered his men to move toward the 642 blockhouses, pillboxes and other gun positions previously identified and shelled through naval barrages—now all silent. The high and soft black dunes slowed the American advance; tanks, heavy machinery and men sank with each step. As Basilone and his men struggled up the beach, the Japanese defenses were waiting quietly. The New Jersey

The view Basilone likely had minutes before disembarking on Iwo Jima. *Library of Congress.*

man who would one day have movies made about him and his name gracing military bases and naval ships undoubtedly thought of his beautiful wife, Lena, as he grasped his machine gun and moved closer to danger. It was all just too quiet—until it was not.

The fire rained down on the marines, kicking up the black sand around them, soon to be stained with the blood of twenty-five thousand Americans. The nearest pillbox quickly pinned down Manila Jack's unit, but this was nothing new to the Raritan man, who had been in worse situations than this one. Basilone signaled to his men to stay back and rushed like a cannonball toward the Japanese position. The man who told his mother that he joined the Marine Corps because "the army isn't tough enough for me" was now making his way around the Japanese position. The men inside did not have a moment to question the daring American. Before they realized what was happening, Manila Jack threw grenades into the strong point and unloaded his Tommy machine gun at anything left moving. He emerged out of the pillbox, living up to the motto tattooed on his arm, "Death Before Dishonor."[92] John reloaded his gun and continued up toward a nearby airfield, only to find himself trapped in an enemy minefield with mortar and artillery barrages, breaking all the rules of civilized warfare. As his platoon members dropped to the ground to return fire, Basilone once more stood tall to help guide a nearby tank past the minefield.

Even among the machine gun fire and explosions, one could not miss the tall young man. With his self-effacing manner and movie star good looks, Basilone was already the U.S. government's War Bonds celebrity before landing on Iwo Jima, featured in parades, newsreels and front covers of newspapers.[93] The fact of the matter was, Manila Jack had already fought his war, seen more than an average soldier and survived to tell the tale. His October 1942 exploits in the Battle of Guadalcanal had turned the tide of the battle and earned him the Congressional Medal of Honor and a ticket home. Yet here he was two years later, standing in a minefield of the most infamous battle of the Pacific War. The Marine Corps offered him a commission and a desk job, which he promptly declined. "I ain't no officer, and I ain't no museum peace," Basilone commented. "I belong with my outfit."[94] Within a year, he was voluntarily back in the Pacific; within minutes, he would never leave it.

With the tank relatively out of danger and the barrage coming down fast and heavy, Manila Jack decided that it was time to move his platoon. "Come on, you guys, we got to get these guns off the beach!" he yelled back—his last words.[95] The mortar shell hit its target accurately.

THE UNPLEASANT TASK OF conveying the community condolences to the marine hero's parents fell to Raritan mayor James J. Del Monte and Reverend Amedeo Russo of St. Ann's Church.[96] They brought a doctor, just in case the occasion proved too much for the elderly couple. All schools in Bridgewater Township sent their student council members to place the schools' American flags at half-staff. The streets looked much different from when John Basilone returned home a Medal of Honor hero of Guadalcanal in September 1943. Back then, the roads in Somerville and Raritan were lined with fifty thousand spectators to watch the parade honoring the only enlisted marine wearing the nation's highest military award.[97] Dubbed "John Basilone Day," the celebrations led Raritan Township to bring its War Savings Bonds' sale total to $1,398,000, with $173,000 coming in within the duration of the parade.[98] The mayor, referring to the success of Sergeant Basilone's ten-day war bond tour for the Treasury Department, now culminating in Manila Jack's hometown, proclaimed, "Sgt. Basilone has come home not only in a blaze of glory but as an inspiration to you and me."[99] The crowd erupted in cheers. Mayor Del Monte might have been thinking back to that day as he rang the doorbell at 113 First Avenue. Mrs. Salvatore Basilone opened the door. She knew why the men were there.

Sergeant John Basilone receives Somerset County's Gift of $5,000 in war bonds from Judge George Allgair during his post–Medal of Honor tour. *From the* Daily Home News, *1943.*

EIGHTEEN MONTHS EARLIER—OCTOBER 24, 1942. "Colonel, there's about 3,000 Japs between you and me." Sergeant Ralph Briggs telephoned the command post of the 1st Battalion, 7th Marine Regiment, at about 9:30 p.m. on October 24, 1942, to report what he and his scouting party had just seen.[100] The battalion commander had sent Briggs ahead to see if the rumors were true, and now he had his answer, whether he liked it or not. The battle for Guadalcanal in the southern Solomon Islands—or the "Island of Death," as the marines called it—had begun months earlier in August. Eleven thousand men of the 1st Marine Battalion quickly overran Japanese positions and took control of the half-finished airfield crucial to the Japanese military operations in Southeast Asia. Since then, the Japanese navy had bombarded the airstrip, now renamed Henderson Field, all while ground troops harassed marine positions in the hopes of retaking the strategic position. For two months, between August and October, the Imperial Army failed, tried and failed again to regain the region, but undeterred and newly reinforced, they would now try again.

Dusk had finally settled over the tropical island when the first artillery barrage lit up the sky. A marine officer looked at his friend and said, "It looks like this is the night."[101] The shelling subsided, and thousands of Japanese troops supported by tanks poured over the ravine, headed straight for the 1st Battalion defending Henderson Field.

Gunnery Sergeant John Basilone of the 1st Battalion, 7th Marines, 1st Marine Division, had simple orders, at least on paper. The Raritan, New Jersey man commanded two sections of heavy machine gun emplacements. Allowing his position to be overrun by the enemy meant that the men stationed behind him near the airfield would be exposed to a frontal attack without much cover. John could not fail them.

The young Basilone was an energetic child, one of ten kids born to an Italian immigrant family. By the time he was fifteen years old, and with much disappointment to his mother, he skipped high school to become a delivery driver for a local laundromat. Everywhere he went, people noted his outgoing, energetic and sometimes restless personality. In 1934, John enlisted in the U.S. Army at eighteen, sending him to Manila in the Philippines, where he became the army's boxing champion and earned the nickname of Manila Jack.[102] After an honorable discharge in 1937, and with the United States and the world not yet at war, John Basilone returned home and back to driving a truck for a living. In 1940, the handsome and tall twenty-four-year-old Italian American enlisted in the Marine Corps. Within two years, the United States was at war with Japan, and Manila

The horrors of the Battle for Solomon Islands are on full display as wounded soldiers are transferred through the jungle to field hospitals. *Library of Congress.*

Jack was back in the Philippines, fighting in the first major American land offensive in the Pacific War.

While the marines had held on to the regained territory near Henderson Field since August 1942, the recent naval defeat to the Japanese Imperial Navy near the island had temporarily stifled the Americans' food supply. Basilone and the 1st Battalion's time defending the airfield was nothing short of miserable, with tropical diseases and malnutrition as dangerous as the constant Japanese attacks. If one asked any Guadalcanal veteran about their experience, he would most likely mention the lack of food and the constant daily rations of the maggot- and worm-infested rice issued by the 1st Marine Division's cooks. If it was any conciliation, the chefs ate the same unappetizing two-tablespoon meal day after day from August to November 1942.[103] Like all those around him, the hot and humid weather, stress of combat, bouts of diarrhea and lack of proper nutrition had turned the ordinarily muscular Manila Jack into a scrawny marine in just a few months. The malaria-carrying mosquitoes were a constant nuisance, if not a downright threat to one's life—especially if the men did not take the military's prescribed medication because of false rumors that it made men sterile. Sergeant Basilone could not miss the damage around him if he tried. Tropical diseases, of which malaria was one of many, disabled two-thirds of the 1st Marine Division, while wounds caused by enemy fire accounted for only one-third of all disabled men on Guadalcanal.[104]

On the night of October 24, 1942, Manila Jack—likely feeling miserable— lay in his humid, hot and mosquito-infested machine gun emplacement when the Japanese launched their latest attack. Basilone's Company C was front and center as artillery, grenades and heavy machine gun fire came down on them without breaks for hours at a time. His sixty men soon dwindled to fewer than thirty and then down to a handful by first light the following day—still, the battle continued. It soon became apparent to the boys of Company C that this Japanese attack was somehow different—more organized, vigorous and relentless. The Japanese general in charge of the assault was sure that his latest overwhelming attack would dislodge the marines from controlling the airfield. Even before firing the artillery barrage, he assigned his staff to begin preparations for accepting the surrender of all American forces defending Guadalcanal.[105]

Bursts of gunfire, screams and piercing machine gun rounds broke the stillness of the dark of night across the American perimeter. The Japanese kept on coming, sometimes so close to the emplacements that their dead bodies blocked the Americans' line of fire. Basilone, who learned the ins and outs of the .30-caliber machine gun during his time with the army, was now running from gun nest to gun nest, repairing jammed machine guns, bringing ammo and encouraging his men.[106] Because of the darkness and overall disarray caused by the oncoming Japanese forces, Manila Jack had to dodge friendly fire as much as that of the Imperial Army. And while he initially dragged dead enemy soldiers' bodies out of the line of fire, he soon had to do the same to his fellow marines who began piling up within the gun nests.

By the time the attack seemed to stop at 1:00 a.m., Basilone had been fighting for more than three hours and found himself personally manning more and more of his machine guns as his Company C numbers dwindled. The respite was brief, as Japanese artillery opened up on his position along the American perimeter. After fifteen minutes, which must have felt like hours, the shelling finally stopped, only to allow enemy infantry to assault the line again. The Japanese kept coming, with as much determination as when the attack began hours before. Soon, a small Japanese group broke through the American lines and scattered among the marine gun and rifle positions, including Manila Jack's.

Suddenly, Sergeant Basilone looked down and noticed that he was missing a shoe. Yet that was not his biggest problem, nor was the fact that he had not eaten or drunk anything since the morning of the previous day—Company C's guns were all too quiet. Crawling out of his position once more, John made it into a nearby gun emplacement, where a scared young marine sitting in the dirt clenching his M1 Garand rifle informed him that he had run out of .30-caliber machine gun ammo. With Japanese gunfire now coming from all directions and supply lines cut, Basilone stayed low as he

We mentioned
7 a night in a
front --- this is how i
feel as i woke up at midnight

Sgt Howard Brodie
Guadalcanal '43
Horses neck front

A drawing by a veteran of the Battle of Guadalcanal showing a soldier on patrol in a foxhole. *Library of Congress.*

ran and dove headfirst into another position in search of shells. This time, the emplacement's machine gun had jammed. Having another marine cover him, the New Jersey man got to work fixing the gun only to see the fellow soldier fall near his feet from a gunshot wound to the head. For the next few minutes, Basilone used the repaired gun to hold off another attack before moving on to the next, this time empty, gun position.

Manila Jack lost track of time, with only the slightly brightening sky above telling him that he had survived longer than even he could have thought possible. The man crawled and rolled back and forth over the blood- and mud-stained ground, firing one gun and then another until it was just him and a handful of other marines holding the spearhead of the Japanese charge. When the attack seemed to once more subside for a brief period, Basilone used the opportunity to reposition the machine guns closer to his and the survivors' positions by dragging the weapons across from abandoned emplacements. The situation soon became desperate as the guns began overheating, prompting the few men left to fire their rifles and pistols to fend off the banzai attacks coming toward their position. With ammunition critically low, Basilone again left his cover to search for any ammo he could find and bring back to the handful of his men. By the time he returned, most guns were silenced, with only a few marines remaining alive. John resupplied the men with extra ammo and moved back to his original position, where he had begun fighting at 9:00 p.m. the previous night.

Knowing that the line would break with the fall of Basilone's position, the Japanese intensified their attacks on the stubborn gun emplacements, not knowing that they were battling a few men or, in reality, an army of one. Sergeant John Basilone fortified his position by dragging an additional machine gun with him. With the morning soon upon him and bringing the inevitability of exposure, the Raritan man crawled out of his gun nest and pulled in dead enemy soldiers to pile up around his emplacement. As the sun began to rise, Basilone awaited the next assault from his bunker of death—thirty-eight hastily piled dead Japanese soldiers now protecting the one life he had left. Manila Jack repelled attack after attack through the morning hours until all he had left was his pistol and a few rounds in its chamber.

When Marine Corps replacements finally arrived in the afternoon, they found the New Jerseyan bloody, shoeless and exhausted. All around him were death and destruction, as far as the eye could see. Manila Jack and the handful of survivors had annihilated an entire Japanese regiment.[107] When offered to be brought farther inland to Henderson Field for medical care, Sergeant Basilone refused and continued at his post for an additional twenty-four hours without any sleep or food. By October 26, 1942, the Japanese attack had officially failed. Basilone held his line to the very end.

An interrogation session after the battle indicated the reason for the Japanese failure in the fight for Henderson Field. "Why didn't you change

Sergeant John Basilone gets a hero's welcome in his hometown of Raritan in 1943. *From the Plainfield Courier News, 1945.*

tactics when you saw you weren't breaking our line?" the American interpreter asked the prisoner. "Why didn't you shift to a weaker spot?" The prisoner looked up at him and answered, "That is not the Japanese way; the plan had been made, and no one would have dared to change it." Adding, "It must go as it is written."[108] And so it went and kept going, right at the position of a determined New Jersey man, a son of a poor Italian tailor, who inspired his men to fight and whose name and deeds would be placed along those of the greatest heroes in American history.

When granted the opportunity to have President Franklin D. Roosevelt personally present him with the Medal of Honor in May 1943, John Basilone instead chose to have the ceremony in the field with his unit. "Only part of this medal belongs to me," he stated. "Pieces of it belong to the boys who are still on Guadalcanal."[109] One year later, having just completed a War Bond tour of the States, the hero of the Solomon Islands said to his new bride, whom he met and married in July 1944, "I'm becoming a museum piece. And what if some marines should land on Dewey Boulevard and Manila John isn't among them?"[110]

On Monday, February 19, 1945, the American forces hit the beaches of Iwo Jima island, 750 miles off the coast of Japan, fast and hard....

# EAGLE AGAINST THE SUN

Usually, nobody noticed the small white house on Cedar Road in Lindenwold, New Jersey. Yet the fire and smoke raging from its second-story window changed everything. It was an otherwise pleasant late afternoon on Wednesday, April 10, 1963, with people just about to sit down for supper. But now, several onlookers stood anxiously looking at the suburban home—some presumably thinking of the latchkey thirteen-year-old Thomas Scott and four of his younger siblings who lived there.

He heard the borough fire siren shortly before 6:00 p.m. from the rear window of his home. By the time he looked outside, the smoke was already rising above the trees a block away. The forty-three-year-old former Lindenwold mayor Carlton R. Rouh threw on his shoes and rushed out the door.

"There's no one home. I called the fire company!" yelled one of the onlookers.[111] But Rouh was not convinced. Coming up the front steps, the World War II veteran forced open the porch window and tumbled into the living room. The darkness and smoke engulfed him. Carlton covered his face with his shirt and scanned the room. The boy lay stretched out halfway up the stairs to the second floor. Feeling like he could not take in any air and was about to pass out, Rouh scooped up the boy in his arms and ran outside.

Falling on the front lawn, the former marine shook the boy. "Where are the other children?" The young man opened his eyes and mumbled, "It's almost out." Rouh continued to jolt the boy, "Where are they?" Young Thomas Scott opened his eyes, "They are next door.…I took them next door."[112]

# Lindenwold Boy Saved From Fire By Marine Hero

By CANDY HIRSCHMANN and LOUIS SCHEINFELD

Lindenwold Marine hero Carlton R. Rouh, who threw himself on a Jap grenade to save the lives of three buddies in 1944, became a hero once again Wednesday night.

The 43-year-old holder of the Silver Star and Medal of Honor forced his way into a burning house and carried to safety an unconscious 13-year-old boy who was suffocating from smoke inhalation.

Lindenwold Police Chief Frank O'Keefe said the boy, Thomas Scott, recovered at Our Lady of Lourdes Hospital and admitted setting the blaze in his second-floor rear bedroom at 409 Cedar

CARLTON R. ROUH

The headline from Camden's *Courier Post* said it all. *From the* Courier Post, *1963.*

Carlton Rouh sat back on the lawn and let the boy rest in front of him. The three fire companies arrived together. The firefighters got to work around him—hoses spread out like snakes across the otherwise pristine grass, now trampled into the mud below by countless footprints. The paramedics took the boy into the ambulance, yet the former captain of the 1st Battalion, 5th Marines, 1st Marine Division, just sat there as men ran to and fro around him, yelling commands. His eyes locked on the wet mud by his feet—the heat of the fire still on his face. Someone was talking to him, but he did not hear them; Captain Rouh was already elsewhere.

PELELIU OF THE PALAU Islands in the Western Pacific was hot, humid and perpetually wet. The rain came down just hard enough on September 14, 1944, to make the next day's humidity push the temperature to 115 degrees Fahrenheit. First Lieutenant Carlton Robert Rouh and the remainder of the 1st Marine Division loaded onto the flat-bottom vessels, which would transport them past the fringing reef that surrounded their latest objective. The men were about to make the small island infamous in the annals of American military history by dying in numbers never before or since seen in any other United States military amphibious assault operation.[113]

Ahead of the men was a fortress unlike any other. As was often the case during the American "Island Hopping" campaign to regain control of the Pacific from the Japanese, Peleliu was chosen due to its enemy airfield, which was dangerous to the American advance. Still, as much as the objective remained the same, this newest amphibious assault would be unlike any other. The island was made up of jagged coral ridge lines, honeycombed with natural caves, which the Japanese had improved into an impregnable defensive line. Farther up the shore, the larger cave fortresses contained electricity, ventilation, stairs and radio communication—one marine would tally "nine staggered levels and so many entrances that it was all but impossible to count them."[114]

The men were tired. The promised rest and recuperation (R&R) in Australia following the Guadalcanal Campaign did not materialize. Instead, the twenty-three-year-old Lindenwold resident and his brothers in arms spent the lead-up to D-Day on the island of Pavuvu, "a rain-soaked, rat-infested hunk of real estate."[115] None of that mattered anymore. The massive naval bombardment that always preceded these invasions continued its assault inland as the Underwater Demolition Teams finished up clearing the shoreline approaches. For good measure, fighter aircraft from nearby U.S. naval carriers had just rained a last-minute hailstorm of bullets on the shoreline defenses. "Nothing could live through that," spoke up one marine.[116] His words could not be any more wrong. Untouched by the initial attack, eleven thousand Japanese waited in their well-conceived natural bunkers.

The landing crafts hit the rough beachhead to the Imperial Army's answer to the bombardment in the form of relentless mortar fire and shelling. As Carlton Rouh went farther up the beach, his feet kept slipping in the knee-high water. Machine gun fire was relentless, seemingly coming from everywhere and nowhere simultaneously. The enemy was there one moment and then gone the next. "The terrain was abominable," recalled one marine. "It was as though several submerged reefs had been forced up out of the water with their jagged edges making several ridges that were up to two or three hundred feet high."[117] The sharp edges of the ground around them cut the Americans' clothing and shoes—falling seemed almost as dangerous as standing up to the bullets.

The smoke from the initial barrage continued to hang low as Rouh and the rest of his 1st Battalion made their way inland. The enemy's hidden gun emplacements took out most of the tanks and armored vehicles sent to provide the infantry some cover. Moving through the pockmarked rock, the men could stand only so much as machine gun fire whizzed past their heads from every direction, including up. Everywhere one looked there were "arms, legs, heads, guts, and brains," recalled one of Rouh's battalion members. Still, the men moved into the "nightmare of flashes, violent explosions, and snapping bullets," impeded by the enemy's pillboxes, blockhouses and cave bunkers.[118]

Rouh looked around at the spread-out, discarded equipment and burning vehicles—and bodies, mangled bodies everywhere. Nearby, a marine stumbled forward, his face a bloody pulp, holding his other severed arm in one hand as if it were a large stick.[119] Pinned down by the incoming fire, one of Lieutenant Rouh's men pointed to a nearby enemy dugout as a place for cover. Another marine equipped with a flamethrower came right by them— seemingly the best way to rid the rivets of enemy soldiers, provided one could find them. The New Jersey man ordered his subordinate to throw a

Carlton Rouh survived shielding a grenade with his body during World War II. *Congressional Medal of Honor Society.*

grenade into the nearby dugout before moving in and setting up a mortar position. Still, something did not seem right. Carlton reached out and grabbed the fellow marine's arm—*not yet.*

Perhaps the Lindenwald man had that same bad feeling he did two years before when he earned a Silver Star for helping evacuate a wounded colleague in Guadalcanal from under heavy enemy fire. The bullet that tore through his chest then took a long time to heal. Maybe he thought of his childhood sweetheart, Phyllis, an army nurse he reconnected with and married while recovering in a hospital in Australia.[120] Still yet, perhaps he thought of nothing at all. Rouh dropped into the dugout, still smoking from the previous grenade explosion. The indescribable pain was back; this time, the bullet hit his side. Carlton fired his rifle—five shots in succession—and, not wasting a moment, began crawling out of the hole, leaving a trail of blood behind him.

Two men grabbed Rouh by the arms and pulled him away from the dugout. The shells continued to rip overhead, shrapnel filling the air around them, machine gun bullets fighting for their place among the mayhem. The New Jersey man was finally far enough away for his men to sit him up against a ridge and begin working on his wound. Men continued tumbling around them, falling where they stood, sometimes in one piece, mostly not. Rouh felt the heat from a soldier's flamethrower, rushing to the crater from which he barely escaped with his life. His blood mixed with mud—all around him mud, fire and blood. And then he heard the splash. With all the strength he had left, First Lieutenant Rouh threw himself at his two men and pushed them aside. He crawled toward the Japanese grenade with all the determination he could muster.[121] Just another foot—almost there. Carlton huddled the object.

The burst ripped his body wide open. Sergeant Ward Walker rushed toward Rouh just quick enough to see the man struggling—the smell of burned flesh and blood filling his nostrils. The New Jersey man, miraculously still breathing, reached out toward the young marine sergeant. In between coughing up blood, Rouh asked, "Are the men all right?"[122] He did not hear the answer.

The Battle of Peleliu continued for nine more weeks, with 40 percent of all Americans fighting for the island suffering wounds or dying in battle. In the end, the National Museum of the Marine Corps called it "the bitterest battle of the war for the Marines," as its airfield proved to be of lesser strategic value than initially expected.[123]

Carlton Rouh woke up in an Australian hospital a few days after the action that should have killed him; he spent the next two years moving from hospital to hospital, fighting for a new lease on life. In 1945, President Harry S Truman presented him with the Congressional Medal of Honor for his action on Peleliu. After the war, the now Captain Routh moved back to his hometown of Lindenwald, New Jersey, and started a family. He died in the safety of his home in 1977—to his townsfolk and family, twice a hero.

GEORGE BENJAMIN JR. OF Carney's Point, New Jersey, was fulfilling General Douglas MacArthur's promise—they all were. The twenty-five-year-old Temple University graduate and employee of the DuPont chemical plant back in his home state pushed ahead. With him were the men of Company A, 306th Infantry, 77th Infantry Division, all moving at a walk, their shoulders hunched over, their bodies inclined and their eyes on the line of broken-off palm trees, where enemy fire raised hell.[124]

They had always said that the war would be over by Christmas, and on this December 21, 1944, it sure seemed like, once again, they were wrong. The Battle of Leyte had started more than two months prior as part of an operation to retake the Philippines and free its people from nearly three years under Japanese occupation. Since capturing the islands in early 1942, controlling the area was still vital to the Imperial armed forces in 1944, as it shielded all major oil supply routes to Japan. For the Americans, reclaiming the islands was a point of pride and strategy. After being ordered off the Philippines following the attack on Pearl Harbor, American general Douglas MacArthur vowed to one day return. It was now that time, and the cameras were ready to record the moment for posterity. But returning to the Philippines and regaining control of the islands from the Japanese were two different things.

He was a radio operator in a somewhat secure position in the rear of the advancing forces, yet Private First Class George Benjamin could never really feel safe. The battle for the Philippines was in its second month of fighting against Japanese resistance when Benjamin and his company came upon a well-defended Japanese strong point. The advance stalled almost immediately, and any movement would mean death from hundreds of projectiles and bullets now cutting through the tropical foliage around them.

Private First Class George Benjamin spearheaded an assault on the enemy lines in Leyte, Philippine Islands. *Congressional Medal of Honor Society.*

The New Jersey man's eyes remained on one of the light tanks continuing ahead, the only means of cover for his rifle platoon. Staying back was not an option, yet the farther the tank got, so did their ability to push forward. Benjamin did not possess a rifle, as did his fellow soldiers; the bulky radio almost permanently attached to his back was enough of a weight to carry. He looked around at his men crouching low to the ground and heads turned in, so all one could see was the tops of their helmets. Benjamin then looked at the tank and took out his pistol, the only weapon he had.

The bullets whizzed past him, some striking his radio. Still, the private first class ran ahead toward the tank, shouting for his men to follow. Before he ever made it to the tank, Benjamin fell into an enemy machine gun emplacement—a shock as much to him as to the few men operating its machine gun. The standard-issue M1911 pistol might as well have been a cannon in the small quarters. The gun's projectiles ripped into the three Japanese soldiers before they knew to pick up their rifles. There was no sense staying in the foxhole, especially now that the surrounding enemy soldiers saw him entering it. George reloaded his pistol and climbed out of the ground. The sacrifice worked; Company A was now moving behind him. The tank was still ahead, the only means for genuine cover, so Benjamin continued his single-man charge forward.

A Japanese soldier came at him with a rifle, and once more, George did not hesitate to pull the trigger of his trusted M1911. The men were now following him—the tank so close he could almost reach it. Another shot came from his left, and Private Benjamin once more used his pistol to silence it. He might not have heard the shot nor felt its impact as he ran, but then his legs gave out and he fell face-first, the heavy radio on his back pushing him deeper into the dirt. The father of two young children back home did not have long to live.

Fellow soldiers reached him almost instantly, took off the heavy radio, and dragged him to the back of the advance and away from enemy fire. All the while, the New Jersey man continued pleading with the medic to see a battalion operations officer. Seeing that Benjamin would not give in and realizing that any more strain would not help his cause, the medic finally obliged. Benjamin slipped in and out of consciousness as the medic held a plasma bottle above his head. In his last moments, the private first class gave his report on the enemy positions he encountered during his forward charge. The officer was still taking notes when he realized that the man had long stopped speaking.

Private Benjamin's young widow accepted her husband's posthumous Congressional Medal of Honor with calm and dignity in a simple ceremony at his place of work back in New Jersey. Perhaps she was sad by her husband's passing, overcome with emotion or simply unwilling to believe that their beautiful young children would never get to know their father.

"FRANK IS AN ALL-AROUND American boy, and as a kid, there was always a twinkle in his eye in spite of his quiet, unassuming manner," the newspapers would later write. "Yet, above all, he is a good Marine and a darn swell fellow."[125] At eighteen years old in 1943, Frank Earl Sigler of Little Falls, New Jersey, knew that enlisting in the Armed Forces was a forgone conclusion. Three of his brothers were already overseas fighting, one having just lost his life. Back home, his kid sister and brother continued helping the war effort through volunteer work and scrap drives.

Frank ached to enlist but worried how it would affect his ailing mother. His "best girl" had still not recovered since the death of his elder brother, Private First Class William C. Sigler. In the end, he did his best to stick around—as best as he could, until finally, he simply could not. With only months left in his senior year of high school, Frank Sigler walked into a local Marine Corps recruitment office without informing his parents of his decision. He began his boot training one month later, in April 1943, and shipped overseas one year later, in July 1944. His parents did not hear from him until September 1945, when a letter written by somebody else on his behalf and signed with an "X" informed them that he had been hurt but was doing better. Within a week, more information came their way about their son's actions in the Pacific. To those who knew Frank Sigler, none of it was surprising.

The local baseball star was the town's favorite. If local folks did not know Frank from his newspaper bicycle route when he was still a preteen, they definitely knew of the middle Sigler since 1939. At the tender age of fifteen, young Frank became a local celebrity when he jumped in after a drowning child in a local pool and managed to revive her before any medical help arrived. The following year, the townspeople collectively held their breath when their "hero" lay an inch away from death after crashing through a car

Frank Sigler led a one-man assault on well-entrenched enemy positions in the bloody fight to take control of the island of Iwo Jima. *Congressional Medal of Honor Society.*

windshield in an automobile accident.[126] Now, five years later—and nineteen months since he enlisted—Little Falls, New Jersey, would once more praise his name.

The telegram arrived from Washington at the doorstep of 5 Clove Road on the last day of September 1945. President Harry S Truman would personally honor Mr. and Mrs. George H. Sigler's son with the Congressional Medal of Honor for his distinguished actions on Iwo Jima. Yet because the twenty-year-old Sigler was still not well enough to travel, the telegram stated, the award would be presented to his family instead. The elder couple still had no idea what their son had done to deserve such recognition. It probably did not even excite them that they would meet the U.S. president in a few weeks.

To Mrs. Sigler, all that mattered was that she did not lose another one of her boys to this terrible war. Frank would be coming home a hero, but more importantly, he would be coming home.

THE BATTLE FOR Iwo Jima continued, now for nearly four weeks. And still the heavily fortified Japanese refused to surrender. In just two days, on March 16, 1945, the American High Command would declare the island secure—all but a seven-hundred-yard-long gorge stronghold at the northwestern end of the island. That job was left to the 5th Marine Division—Private Franklin Earl Sigler of the 26th Marines, 2nd Battalion, not excluded. Admiral Nimitz might have proclaimed that "all powers of the government of the Japanese Empire in these islands are hereby suspended" and that Iwo Jima was officially secured; still, the young New Jerseyan continued seeing men lose their lives all around him.[127] The marines continued inching forward, killing and dying. On March 11, two companies covered barely twenty-five yards to the tune of thirty-three casualties; on the twelfth, they were stalled and added another twenty-seven losses—it had become that kind of war.[128]

The naval support coming from nearby destroyers became so commonplace that the Americans hardly noticed the noise and the overhead shells that filled the sky day in and day out. Still, the U.S. marine infantry continued moving toward their ultimate goal of securing the entirety of the island.

The problem lay in the hidden pockets of resistance and well-coordinated Japanese attacks, a departure from chaotic enemy banzai charges the marines had previously experienced. Iwo Jima had become a battle of yards and feet. Tanks were put out of action by mines, suicide squads or well-camouflaged antitank guns, all while the marine rifle companies, such as Sigler's Company F, were continuously subjected to artillery, mortar and small-arms fire.[129] Like the men around him, young Sigler did not see much of the enemy, who were often entrenched and well hidden underground. "They would wait for the Marine lines to pass by their positions, then they would pop up behind you and take a crack at you," a marine with Sigler's division later recalled. "It was like fighting ghosts," he added. "The entire time I was there, I only saw two or three Japanese, and they were dead or wounded."[130] Often a trapdoor would open, and Japanese artillery would unleash projectiles toward the Americans. Before anyone could figure out where the fire had come from, the trapdoor was closed and indistinguishable from the rock face.

As Frank Sigler and the other members of the 2nd Squad, 3rd Platoon, Company F, continued their advance toward the remaining Japanese stronghold, temporary American cemeteries multiplied directly behind them. Each day was the same, going out on patrol to find the enemy, and each day coming back with fewer men than the group set out with that morning. The island was scraggly and cold; sometimes, on patrol, the men would notice volcanic steam seeping out of nearby rocks, which often made a perfect heat to warm up their K-rations. And although most of the defenses they encountered were underground, thousands of machine gun pillboxes were

American marines land on the black sands of Iwo Jima. Mount Sirubahi, which the Japanese turned into a fortress, overlooks their advance. *Library of Congress.*

scattered around the island—each with a small slit in the wall through which the enemy would fire on the oncoming marines. "I saw some of the most heroic actions here," a marine said in a later interview. "These kids, I called them kids because they weren't much older than that, would charge up these pillboxes. They'd jump on the top and throw a satchel charge through the slit right before they'd get hit by another machine gun."[131] One of these kids he spoke about was Little Falls' Private Francis Sigler.

March 14, 1945, began much like any other day on Iwo Jima for Private Sigler—fighting the enemy and the island with its numerous traps, caves and hidden pillboxes. Men could tell that once this "bloody gorge" fell, so would the last opposition on the island, and the marines were willing to do anything to see it through to the end. The fire opened unexpectedly, and Sigler's rifle company found itself without a commanding officer. Unwilling to stay pinned down by the machine gun, the twenty-year-old private took command and ordered the men to fall in behind him as he led them forward from one large rock to another, all while avoiding the open ground in front of the pillbox. Frank peeked out from behind his shelter and located the small slit in what otherwise looked like another rock formation. The private in command looked at the two men near him and signaled them with his hand to cover him, took a deep breath and left his cover.

Sigler stayed low as he charged the pillbox, his hands clenching the grenades like they once did baseballs when he played for his high school team. The marine never broke his stride as he threw the explosives into the bunker's small opening while throwing himself past it on the ground. The explosion shook the ground under him. Sigler stood back up and looked back at his men, but before he could signal them that all was clear, the mountainous caves above him opened fire. Sigler briefly threw himself on the ground before deciding to run toward the enemy instead of retreating to his rifle company's position. Facing the invisible enemy still seemed the better choice than turning his back on it. Once at the base of the hill, Frank looked up and located a few secret openings above him. He searched his bag for more grenades and began scaling the wall after finding three more explosives. The machine gun fire now continued from new positions behind him, yet the man continued until he silenced two more enemy posts. Perhaps around this time, he realized that he had been shot multiple times—or maybe he did not.

The young man crawled back to his rifle squad, whose men, in awe of what they had just seen, covered his return with all the firepower and courage they could muster. Pulled into the safety of a natural rock wall by another marine, Sigler asked for his rifle and continued assaulting the Japanese

American marines hurl grenades at Japanese positions during the Island Hopping Campaign in the Pacific. *Library of Congress.*

position instead of allowing the medic to look over his wounds. The situation around him quickly deteriorated, with some men sprawled out near Sigler's feet, bleeding out from open wounds. Knowing that the young man now looking up to him from the dirty ground would soon die, Private Sigler put down his rifle and, ignoring his own pain, scooped up the wounded soldier and carried him away from the fighting and toward the back line. He then rushed back to his rifle company's position, only to see another young boy mortally wounded. "Undaunted by the merciless rain of hostile fire," Sigler picked up the wounded man and rushed him back to the awaiting medics. The New Jersey man repeated the action once more before finally collapsing and losing consciousness from his own wounds.

The Battle of Iwo Jima ended a little more than a week after Private Sigler's heroic actions. Around the same time, the New Jersey man woke up in an army hospital, vaguely recalling what he had done. And even when he remembered, Frank never put too much stock in his actions—he was just doing what anybody else would have done in his position. Even after finally being able to communicate with his family in the States, Sigler would not comment on that day on Iwo Jima. He did have the person writing for him say that he was hurt and that "the future doesn't look good."[132] The Siglers of Little Falls learned most of what had transpired from Frank's buddies, writing that he had been severely injured, which included injuries to his hands that made him unable to write. Frank's secondhand letters also did not mention that he had been awarded the Purple Heart.

One week before his parents received the telegram that informed them of their son's Medal of Honor citation, Frank's sixteen-year-old sister, Mildred, received a letter from one of their mutual marine friends telling her that her older brother had done something extraordinary. Yet to the family back in New Jersey, the only extraordinary thing that Frank accomplished, and the only thing that mattered, was that he survived.

A bridge over the Passaic River at the junction of Little Falls, Totowa and Wayne now bears the name of the Iwo Jima veteran who came home to continue helping his community and those he cared about. Frank had become a Little Falls police officer and later a detective—a hero 'til the end.

# COVERING FIRE

They called him "Pops." Even though he was only twenty-nine years old, Stephen R. Gregg of Bayonne, New Jersey, was the youngest man in his unit of boys and faced dangers other men could never imagine in their lifetimes.[133] For a man whom the government excused from fighting due to his position as a naval dockyard worker, Stephen could not allow himself to take the easy way out. Just days after the Japanese attack on Pearl Harbor on December 7, 1941, the humble and modest Gregg stood in line for his physical with hundreds of thousands of American volunteers. Assigned to the 143rd Infantry Regiment of the 36th Infantry Division, the dockworker sailed for Algeria on April 2, 1943. Within months he would find himself fighting in Italy. Gregg began his journey toward being immortalized in the annals of American military history—he just did not know it yet.

While the Italians withdrew from fighting, the Germans were more than willing to defend Italy. The Americans suffered significant losses from the onset, especially without any preceding naval bombardments, a decision made to achieve the element of surprise. Having survived the bloody landings, Gregg and the rest of the 36th Division moved fairly uneventfully upward through the Italian peninsula. The Bayonne man's memories of his time in Italy mainly were of monotony, not the horror of war. "It constantly rained during the eleven months [I was there], often in muddy foxholes watching German and American artillery duels overhead."[134] Then came the infamous Winter Line and the Battle of Rapido River— the day Pops met war.

The Allies' advance through Italy stalled in January 1944 at a series of Axis military fortifications in and around the town of Monte Cassino, known as the German Winter Line. The orders came for Sergeant Gregg's 143rd Infantry to cross the Gari River via boats and seize control of the western bank to make progress against the impregnable German lines. Landmines left on shore would cause the majority of the initial American deaths before the enemy artillery rained down on the American infantry. Gregg's rifle company was one of two that managed to gain a foothold on the opposite shore, albeit briefly. The German gunfire was relentless enough to push them back. By the next day, after another failed attempt, the casualties were too high to justify another try. Gregg's leg wound sustained during the crossing led to one of the first medals of his career and one he probably could have lived without: a Purple Heart. Finally relieved in late February, Stephen's division was prepped and sent over to Anzio to help secure Rome. By the end of that tour of duty, Pops would add a Silver Star to his medals. For many other veterans, Gregg's wartime record thus far would be the end of the story they would tell their grandkids. For Technical Sergeant Stephen Gregg, it was only the beginning.

THE MEN KNEW THAT this was no Normandy of three months prior, but they were still getting their chance of invading France and helping to end this darn war. Operation Dragoon, or the invasion of southern France in August 1944, would become relegated to the back of history books, especially in light of Operations Overlord and Market Garden. But to the men of the 143rd, now tasked with blocking the weakened German retreat through the town of Montelimar, this was still war.

It is incredible how much strength and fury arises within an organism when cornered without a way out of inevitable danger—nothing compares to the fight for survival. Instead of forcing the Germans to open another front and divert some armies to southern France, Operation Dragoon caused a desperate exodus of German units from the area. A race against time ensued between the German Army Group G and the U.S. forces attempting to cut them off. Allowing Hitler's forces to escape back to Germany to fight another day was not an option.

An American taskforce was hastily sent to hold a 250-square-mile sector in and around Montelimar that included two-thousand-foot-high hills overlooking farmland. When the Germans arrived, the small American command tasked with keeping the area found itself confronted by two

German corps frantic to escape. The American force trying to stop them included barely thirty Shermans, a dozen tank destroyers, an infantry battalion and twelve self-propelled guns.[135] Already short of supplies, the grossly outmatched Americans were barely holding on when the infamous German 11th Panzer Division came in to reinforce its armed withdrawal. The area was home to attacks and counterattacks for the next seventy-two hours, with both sides unwilling to yield.

Gregg's 143rd Division arrived in Montelimar three days later, on August 23, 1944, as part of the 36th Infantry. By then, the German battle for survival reeked of desperation—with many men fighting to the death desperately trying to escape. The New Jersey man and his weapons platoon of Company L were fighting a chaotic battle with German sniper and artillery attacks, giving way only to ferocious enemy infantry charges. By the end of the first day of fighting, the 36th Division, which managed to surround the German 19th Army, was itself surrounded. The German forces had breached both flanks by August 25. One soldier later remembered the Panzers being "so close you could feel the heat from their motors."[136]

On August 25, a charge of six German battle groups was so intense that a U.S. battalion commander called artillery onto his own post to avoid being overrun—all to no avail.[137] The 11th Panzer Division punched a hole through the American lines, pouring its convoys past it and to the north in an organized retreat. The fighting continued, with neither side admitting surrender. The Americans turned the hill area around Montelimar into its central defensive position, but it now seemed like they would not be able to hold it much longer against the oncoming German desperation. The hill was now covered with burning and exploding tanks, knocked-out guns and dead men.[138]

The rain pelted Sergeant Gregg's helmet all day on Sunday, August 27, but it was still better than what the Germans must have felt from the 2,500 mortar rounds the artillery had dropped on their positions since the morning. The Bayonne man and fellow soldiers watched the shellfire grow so furious that the road asphalt caught fire.[139] As far as the brass was concerned, the barrage was working; the German advance past Montelimar was stalling. For Gregg and his men on the ground, it meant a desperate and cornered enemy and a difficult night. They did not have to wait too long. Two German columns of the 198th Division attempted to sneak past the Americans as they ran into the 143rd Infantry shortly after nightfall. Within minutes, bodies covered the wet ground and blood mixed with the pouring rain—the road no longer passable. Gregg and his men of Company L fought bitterly through

Lieutenant Stephen R. Gregg was awarded the Medal of Honor for his actions in Southern France. *Congressional Medal of Honor Society.*

the orchards and scrub woods as the nearby 132nd Field Artillery Battalion opened fire at the German columns stacked bumper to bumper, the shells chopping them all into pieces.[140]

Gregg kept his distance behind the leading scouts of his platoon. It was dark, but the artillery explosions around them provided just enough light. The sound of men shrieking in terror pierced through the gunfire, both in German and English. The Germans appeared out of nowhere, their fire finding its mark. The platoon point men dropped like dead weight. The technical sergeant from New Jersey fell and buried his face behind the .30-caliber M1919 Browning machine gun. He flicked out the tripod, found his mark and opened fire. All around him, the remaining platoon members used whatever terrain they could to stay low. Gregg fired the machine gun past the wounded scouts and the small detachment of men attempting to charge the German position. The M43s, more commonly known as the German potato masher grenades, ripped into the advancing men, kicking up bodies and dirt as freely as fall winds do with leaves. The shrieks of terror and calls for help from those still alive were more than a person could take and went on without remorse.

Pops lessened the pressure on his trigger and looked ahead at the body of a medic who sacrificed his life trying to get to the wounded men. As he stared at the red cross on the body's arm, the sounds of helplessness beyond seemed to intensify. Thoughts racing through his head, Stephen murmured under his breath, "Okay, what the hell; so I'm never coming back."[141] The man others considered the group's adult leader picked up the heavy Browning machine gun. Its weight forced him to set it on his hip, and its heat burned into his flesh. It no longer mattered. Gregg moved up the hill, firing the heavy weapon from his hip right into the direction of the German line. Two medics followed behind him—just a man and a machine gun standing between them and certain death. Unwilling to risk getting shot, the enemy troops instead blindly threw grenades in the direction of the incoming fire. Still, Pops continued holding the trigger of his M1919 as if his life depended on it. The medics began dragging back the wounded under the New Jerseyan's covering fire, coming back twice to save all seven men.

Gregg's index finger was still on the trigger when the machine gun stopped—his ammo expended. The four enemy soldiers were on him in an instant. "*Hande hoch! Hande hoch! Schnell!*" Pops dropped his machine gun and raised his hands, the handful of Germans now directly around him. Unbeknownst to the Bayonne man, other platoon members had managed to maneuver undetected into closer firing positions while he took all the attention covering the medics with his M1919. Gregg looked right into the German man's eyes before him as a bullet struck the side of the enemy's neck.

The sergeant dropped to the ground along with the three remaining Germans. Without much thought, the American ripped the MP-40 submachine gun from one of the enemy soldiers' hands and began firing as he stood up and ran for cover. The frantic bullets fell on the Germans, killing one and wounding another. When he finally reached his original machine gun position and turned around to fire, the remainder of the enemy was nowhere to be seen. With Gregg in the forefront, Company L crept up the hill to see all German positions abandoned. The area was secure, for now. The men knew that the enemy would try to get out again the next day. With only a few hours left before daybreak, Gregg and his men dug in and set up artillery and defensive positions. All that was left to do was wait for the inevitable.

The sun was not even up when the Germans launched their counterattack. Although not anything they had not seen before, the German Panzers spearheading the Germans' final attempt at a breakthrough intimidated even the most battle-hardened soldier. Members of Company L braced themselves for the attack. Stopping the Germans was out of the question, but perhaps they could delay them just enough for American reinforcements to arrive—all while inflicting as many casualties as possible. Many men would not return from that hill on that day. In charge of a mortar position, Sergeant Gregg spent enough time scouting his hill position and the valley below to calibrate his fire to inflict the most damage. His men did not disappoint.

The Germans moved up the hill toward Company L's entrenchments, only to be picked off by a heavy barrage of American artillery, coordinated from a nearby machine gun position by none other than the Bayonne man. Pops stayed close to his radio and, like an orchestra conductor, directed the sounds of shells filling the sky and hitting their targets. The day seemed long, and while the enemy could trickle past the Americans, Gregg's company made the task much more complicated than it otherwise would have been. By the afternoon, the hungry, dirty and slightly hard-of-hearing Pops had watched his men fire thousands of machine gun rounds. His artillery position farther down the ridge dropped more than six hundred shells on the Germans. But now, as he attempted to relay another message to his artillery section, his radio stayed silent. Things quickly went from bad to worse as mortar shells began falling on his positions along the ridge. Something was not right.

Grabbing a rifle, Gregg left his machine gun embankment with two supporting men, and staying as low to the ground as they could, the men trekked ahead, checking for breaks in the communication wire. The closer they got to the artillery position, the fiercer the heavy small-arms fire became. Someone did not want Gregg and his men to make it to the artillery, and now they knew why. The Germans cut the line at the source, commandeered the mortars and fired them at Company L. As the three men lay there, inching closer to the position, Pops signaled to the two young soldiers to cover him while he set off toward the mortars and the five Germans who now manned them.

There were too many of them for him to try and charge in, so Gregg crawled quietly to the edge of the dug-up position. The Germans did not have enough time to jump out of the way when Pop's grenades hit the ground beneath their feet. The explosion was loud, kicking up smoke, dirt and the mingled body of a German soldier. Before the remaining enemy troops who had survived the blast oriented themselves enough to pick up their weapons, Gregg was already on them, shooting two. When he turned his rifle toward the remaining Germans on the ground, their hands were already up. "*Nicht schieben!*"

The sound of American artillery once more filling the air never sounded sweeter.

By the time the reinforcements arrived and pushed into the town of Montelimar, the Germans were all but gone—behind them were 4,000 burnt-out vehicles and 1,500 dead horses.[142] Although most of the enemy slipped away, Stephen Gregg and his men's actions on August 27 and 28 contributed to the capture of 8,000 Germans. The Bayonne man's Medal of Honor presented to him in March 1945 for his actions during Operation Dragoon's Battle for Monterlimar would be one of the last signed by President Franklin D. Roosevelt before his passing in April of that year.

Stephen R. Gregg returned to Bayonne, New Jersey, a quiet hero in May 1945. He was honored by twelve thousand of his fellow townsmen on May 14 and presented with a check for $1,000 made up of the town's oversubscription to the war bond drive. As fate would have it, it was also the day he met his future wife, Irene, whom he would marry two years later.

Stephen worked for the Hudson County Sheriff's Department for the next fifty years until his retirement and subsequent death in 2005. Many children and adults pass by a bronze statue of Gregg holding a machine gun like the one with which he saved the lives of seven wounded men back in France in 1944. It is located in a park in Bayonne that bears his name, a constant reminder that freedom does not come without sacrifice.

# FINAL BREATH AGAINST THE THIRD REICH

Nobody could tell the boys flying daily missions over Germany in late 1944 that the German air force, the Luftwaffe, was no longer a dangerous and defiant foe—they knew better. Since January 1943, the U.S. Army Air Corps' deadly daylight bombings of Germany had inflicted massive damage to the enemy's ability to continue the fight, all at a terrible cost to American lives. By May 1945, together with the British Royal Air Force, the U.S. 8th Army Air Force dropped nearly fifty-three thousand tons of explosives on Germany monthly. On December 24, 1944, Air Force Mission No. 760, an attack on German airfields, was not out of the ordinary by the standard of the last few months. As the ground war seemed to be trailing off, the air campaign intensified to take advantage of nearly supreme air control over European skies.

Brigadier General Frederick Walker Castle, a graduate of Boonton High School and a Mountain Lakes, New Jersey resident, looked out of the small cockpit window of his B-17 bomber, the *Treble Four*. The gray sky was filled with aircraft everywhere the eye could see—like a swarm of angered bees coming after their target. Castle nodded to his co-pilot, First Lieutenant Robert W. Harriman, and returned to looking at his controls. The Christmas Eve mission was designated as "maximum effort" and involved three air divisions, a total of 2,046 B-17 and B-24 bombers, escorted by 853 fighters.[143] The brigadier general's 487th Bombardment Group H led the 3rd Air Division, a total of 96 bombers and many fighters. Their target: an airfield in Babenhausen, Germany.

Colonel Fredrick W. Castle (*forth from left*) during a post-mission debriefing. *U.S. Air Force.*

The weather was less than ideal, perhaps to be expected for late December. Castle watched freezing rain, fog and snow pelt his windshield. The *Treble Four*'s crew of six officers, three of them sergeant gunners and three navigators, usually stayed a bit more relaxed until their bomber crossed over German territory, where the Luftwaffe and anti-aircraft guns were most determined and deadly. Since the start of the prior week's German offensive (soon called the Battle of the Bulge) in the Ardennes Forest in Belgium, that was no longer the case. Regardless of the elevated Luftwaffe presence in the area they were flying over, it did not detract from the mission, especially that of the *Treble Four*. Castle's B-17 stayed steady at twenty-two thousand feet, leading the entire pack with its rotating antenna in place of a ventral ball turret. As the "Pathfinder," the New Jersey man's aircraft was equipped with H2X ground-mapping radar, allowing a radar navigator to locate a target through cloud cover.[144]

Castle's bomber continued at the head of a tight formation, which placed the bombers close to one another to discourage the German pilots from attacking the squadrons from the rear. Charging attacks put the Luftwaffe at a disadvantage, leaving them with only three to five seconds before being within range of the formation and countless heavy machine gun fire.[145] Frederick Walker Castle was used to the pressure. Born on the Philippine Islands in 1908 to Second Lieutenant Benjamin Frederick Castle (U.S. Army), the younger Castle had spent his entire life around the military. He enlisted in the New Jersey National Guard at sixteen in 1924, graduated from the West Point Military Academy in 1930 and was transferred to the U.S. Air Corps a short year later.[146] His exceptional leadership of the 94th Bombardment Group of the USAAF, with which he won the Silver Star for gallantry, led to a recent promotion to brigadier general on November 20, 1944. Castle received his new rank insignia just a week before Mission No. 760. His mother, back home in Mountain Lakes, New Jersey, would find out about her son's promotion in a few days—along with the notice of his death.

The Battle of the Bulge was waging below them, and the Luftwaffe's Me-109 fighters buzzed around the squadrons just far enough to be out of range of the bomber's machine guns. The temperature outside was sixty degrees below zero. Castle did not have to look at his instrument panel to know that something was wrong, although it soon confirmed that the number four engine on the right wing was losing oil and the B-17 was losing power. The brigadier general had two options, and neither seemed ideal. He could jettison his bomb load to make up the speed by shedding weight or relinquish his lead position and fall behind. Castle undoubtedly looked down thousands of feet below and thought of the countless American troops battling the cold winter and Hitler's most ambitious and violent offensive they had ever seen. The *Treble Four* was directly over the American 1st Army formation, and dropping its full load almost surely meant killing many innocent Americans below. The general decided and pulled back on the throttle—the swarm of Me-109s awaited.

The combat crew of General Castle's *Treble Four*. U.S. Air Force.

The *Treble Four* slowly fell out of formation, with the Luftwaffe coming fast and determined, like hyenas chasing wounded pray. The fighters attacked feverishly, putting two additional B-17 engines out of operation. Castle did not hesitate, and with a visual agreement from co-pilot Harriman, the two men shouted into the onboard intercom for the crew to abandon ship. Maneuvering the aircraft was becoming more difficult by the minute, especially since its right wing was now on fire. The general and Harrington needed to keep the struggling machine in the air long enough for their men to get out. And then he saw them, first one, then another and another. The machine guns from the German Me-109 opened on the parachuters almost immediately. Three of the six men who jumped out would soon touch the ground alive. Three others were not lucky enough to avoid the German bullets. As the last heavily wounded man slowly descended toward the snow-covered Belgian forest, only to soon die from his wounds, the general continued his struggle in the air.

Looking for a proper place to bring his aircraft down to inflict the least damage to any Americans below and contain the inevitable explosion, Castle lowered the *Treble Four* to about twelve thousand feet and ordered Harrington to put on his parachute. The man in the cockpit must have heard and seen the unavoidable conclusion to their struggle before he felt it. The B-17's flaming right wing finally came off with a violent tug, sending the aircraft into a spin. Castle could only hope that his co-pilot got out in time as he himself clenched the controls and attempted the impossible. The heavy machine, proudly built back home in California just three months prior, broke apart like building blocks into several sections. The largest remaining part of the B-17, the forward fuselage—including the bomb bay, left wing and inboard right wing—crashed with indescribable force about three hundred yards from an old castle structure below, Chateaux d'Englebermont, Belgium.[147]

General Castle managed to save the lives of many fellow Americans on the ground. But he never lived to know it. The wreck, with the general still in the cockpit and his co-pilot in the bomb bay, exploded immediately after hitting the ground. It was Harriman's fifty-third mission, after which he was to return home for his wedding. His fiancée's mother would burn all her records of him so she would get on with her life.[148] General Frederick Castle would never return home to Mountain Lakes. Every ten years or so, a federal government representative enters the quaint Mountain Lakes Library in the middle of a quiet, green suburban neighborhood. He enters the back room, uses a specially sanctioned key, opens a glass case, takes out

B-17 Bombers equipped with the H2X Ground Mapping Radar like the one General Castle flew. *U.S. Air Force.*

Castle's Congressional Medal of Honor and cleans it. When he is done, he puts everything back as he found it, bids the library director goodbye and disappears for another ten years.[149]

JOHN AND ELIZABETH MCGRAW stood silently inside the St. Joan of Arc Parish Hall in Camden, New Jersey. It was November 2, 1945, and Major General Leland S. Hobbs, standing beside the elderly couple, spoke to those assembled about what a great man Francis was. Mr. McGraw looked blankly ahead as his hands clenched a small box. The sadness in his eyes said it all.[150] No matter how prestigious the Medal of Honor the general just presented to them, it would not bring back his boy. First, he lost his first wife, Frank's mother, during childbirth, and now he'd lost his son. In two weeks, it would be a year since Francis Xavier McGraw gave his life for his country in Germany, yet the pain his father undoubtedly felt that day might as well have made it yesterday.

They called the unit the "Big Red One" because of its insignia of a large number one on a khaki patch, but there was much more pride behind that for the men of the 1st Infantry Division of the U.S. Army. Organized in June 1917 following America's entrance into the Great War, the men of the 1st knew its significance of being the first permanent division in the Regular Army and often the first one to deploy and engage the enemy during warfare. Frank X. McGraw knew it, as did all other soldiers wearing the famous patch on their shoulders. The twenty-six-year-old Camden man had been with the division since the very beginning—from Algeria in 1942 to Sicily in 1943, then Normandy, France, on June 6, 1944, and now Germany

Major General Hobbs speaks after presenting Mr. and Mrs. McGraw with their son's Medal of Honor. *From the* Courier Post, *1945.*

in November 1944. He survived all the horrors the war presented him with. But that was before. Before the Battle of Hurtgen Forrest, before the descent to the closest the Big Red One ever got to hell on earth—a place the troops would simply call the "Death Factory."

Frank's Company H, 26th Infantry, 1st Infantry Division, had been battling the forest and weather elements and the German army since October to no end. November 1944 had not been much different, except that the cold weather and early snow had made it worse. Instead of growing naturally, the Hurtgen townsfolk had, many years ago, planted the trees that covered the steep hills now surrounding the Americans. The tall forest of twenty by ten miles had since grown so thick it blocked out the sun. "The Hurtgen Forest is a seemingly impenetrable mass," noted an official army document, describing what the private from New Jersey called home for months before his death. "A vast, undulating, blackish-green ocean stretching as far as the eye can see. Upon entering the forest, you want to drop things behind to mark your path, as Hansel and Gretel did with their bread crumbs."[151] In November, one member of the Big Red One called it "a monster, an ice-coated Moloch, with an insatiable capacity for humans."[152]

Private First Class Francis X. McGraw manned a heavy gun emplacement in a foxhole in Germany before being mortally wounded. *Congressional Medal of Honor Society.*

By the time it was over, the Battle of Hurtgen Forest, which began in September and ended in December 1944, had become the longest single battle the U.S. Army had ever fought. Now desperately fighting on German soil, the Germans claimed almost fifty-five thousand American casualties. The forest defenses included miles of minefields, hidden pillboxes, hidden artillery emplacements and countless sniper nests—the Germans were ready. The September and October rains had turned the few narrow roads leading to and from Hurtgen into mud that sucked heavy machinery almost a foot deep below its surface. Without the needed armored support, the American infantry entered alone. Until the temperature dropped and the snow fell a few weeks before, the battlefield resembled the trench warfare of the Great War. But instead of trenches, the Americans lived in foxholes.[153]

Frank McGraw and his fellow Americans were surviving the unimaginable—at least to those reading about the war in the *Saturday Evening Post* in the comfort of their living rooms back home. The three entrenched German divisions poured on the artillery daily, causing broken treetops and branches to pummel down on the men like deadly spears from the skies. The men knew that there was no way out of their foxholes. The hard and freezing soil had replaced the October water that reached their ankles; C-ration cans (into which they sometimes defecated) filled the bottom of each trench. Trying to leave the foxhole into the snow-covered ground meant fulfilling a German sniper's wish.

Private Walter K. Bedillion, another 1st Division, 26th Infantry member, never knew Frank McGraw. However, as fate would have it, he was directly next to him when the Camden man's sacrifice helped Bedillion come home to his wife and baby daughter—albeit paralyzed from the neck down. Day after day, the men struggled for survival. Having dug up their foxholes as quickly as possible when arriving in the forest in late October, Frank McGraw and the other members of his infantry cut down pine tree branches, covered their foxholes and huddled together to keep warm. "The biggest worries were when it began to snow," Bedillion would recall to his grandson years later, "because the area was crawling with Germans that might come along any minute and accidentally step into a foxhole."[154] Private Frank McGraw stayed put in his foxhole through his weeks in the Hurtgen Forest. Each day, the German artillery targeted the treetops above his unit. "[Sometimes] the safest place when we went off [to patrol] was hugging the tree because the artillery literally blew trees apart above us, causing more damage to the people than shrapnel."[155] And even then, if the men ever made it anywhere, they would take ten feet and then lose it, moving from foxhole to foxhole of a fallen comrade.

When the mortar fire started on Sunday, November 19, 1944, Private Bedillion was outside of his foxhole and, together with a friend, dove for the nearest one. A mortar whistled in and exploded above their heads in the treetops, sending chunks of trees and shrapnel in all directions. Surviving the barrage was one thing, but the German infantry advance that always followed at close quarters was another. Still, Bedillion was done fighting for the day. When the hour of shelling was over, he lay beside his dead friend in a frozen foxhole—bleeding profusely from his wounds and only able to move his head. The Germans would be coming any minute. And then he heard the machine gun fire coming from a nearby foxhole. Bedillion lay there in and out of consciousness for the next six hours until the evacuation team and medics made it to him[156]—all while listening to the exploits of the brave American next to him, one he would never know: Private Frank X. McGraw.

The Germans crept up slowly, their white winter overcoats further masked by the snow and the low-hanging fog. McGraw waited just long enough for a few figures to get closer and then put his M1917 Browning heavy machine gun to work. At first, the enemy continued coming, but they soon tired of having to pass by their fallen comrades. The young private was relentless, not giving the Germans an inch of ground until they brought up their heavy machine gun to take him out. Even then, the Camden man refused to be silenced. The severely wounded Private Bedillion lay quietly in a nearby foxhole listening to the German attack falter and then resume, only to once again stop due to the determined man in the nearby position.

To his loved ones back home, Frank McGraw was a very mild-mannered man—that is, unless someone went after his friends or family. His younger siblings would later recall how one could push Frank a mile and get no reaction, but if anyone bothered his siblings, the reaction was always swift and final. As a high school student, McGraw once encountered his younger brother and cousin walking back from a pickup baseball game where they had been chased away by high school bullies. Frank walked back to the field, grabbed the third base from the ground and threw it up on a nearby garage's

The Battle of the Hurtgen Forrest, the longest land battle in U.S. history, still ranks as one of the worst American soldiers ever fought in. *U.S. Army.*

roof. He then turned around and, with a baseball bat in his hand, dared the bullies to go up and retrieve it.[157] If they wanted to play, they would have to first get by him, something they were unwilling to do. Now, four thousand miles away from home, twenty-six-year-old Frank stood his ground again, daring the oncoming Germans to knock him out of position.

As the Germans brought up their machine gun to get rid of the American private once and for all, Frank, exposing himself to the deadly fire, stood up in his foxhole and dragged his heavy gun to a position on a nearby log in front of it. Henceforth standing, McGraw poured fire onto the oncoming Germans, silencing their new machine gun emplacement. Just then, a second machine gun burst out from another direction, and the New Jersey man dealt with it as he had with the previous. The impatient, flustered and angered Germans brought up anti-tank rocket launchers, the Panzerfausts, promptly firing them toward McGraw. The blast that knocked him back and sent his machine gun to the ground came unexpectedly. Yet, undeterred, the slightly shell-shocked private leaped toward his machine gun, sending a firestorm of bullets at the perpetrators. He then repositioned his M1917 Browning once more and continued to repel any oncoming advancements.

"The fire was so intense that the ammunition bearers were unable to cover the short distance to the ammunition dump where supplies were stored in a deep trench," First Sergeant Joseph Baruno later remembered. "I saw Private McGraw make three trips to pile up supplies next to his gun."[158] On his third trip, a burst of machine gun fire hit the Camden man, and he briefly went down, only to get back up and continue to his foxhole. Baruno yelled toward him to stay down and await medical treatment, but McGraw waved him away. He yelled back, "After the enemy stops trying to get through!"[159] Before Frank could return to his machine gun, a German soldier was on him, only for the American to cut him down with his pistol. McGraw was soon back at his post, firing his Browning as further Panzerfaust blasts exploded around him, kicking up snow, dirt and sometimes pieces of human bodies. Yet McGraw continued firing, repositioning and resetting his machine gun each time a nearby explosion knocked it down, until he ran out of ammunition.

With most Germans having given up on trying to pierce through his position, only a few enemy soldiers were still facing McGraw. Frank picked up his M1 Carbine and began firing. His shots found their mark once again, but then so did one coming from the opposite direction—the one that mattered the most, the one that took Frank Xavier McGraw's life.

The telegram delivered to Mr. and Mrs. John McGraw back at 3110 Merrimac Road, Camden, New Jersey, was not unlike the thirty-three thousand others delivered to mothers and fathers nationwide following the brutal fighting at the Hurtgen Forest. "The Secretary of War desires me to express his deep regret that your son Private First Class Francis X. McGraw, was killed in action on Nineteen November in Germany—letter follows."[160]

THE ALLIED ANZIO LANDINGS in Italy dragged on for months since they began in July 1944; it might as well have been years for the American soldiers slugging it out with the German occupants. Anzio sat sixty miles above the stalled Allied offensive in Italy and only thirty-five miles away from Rome. The amphibious landing of more than 110,000 Allied troops behind enemy lines stalled almost instantly upon arrival. The Germans' swift reaction placed the Americans on the defensive, where they virtually remained for the next five months. After weeks of continuous bombing, shelling and fighting, the exhausted American and German armies settled into a stalemate. For the next few months, until early May, both armies limited their operations to defending the already gained positions, all while conducting limited counterattacks and minor raids.[161]

The orders for the final offensive and breakout from the beachhead finally arrived in May. Private First Class John W. Dutko, like the rest of the men of the 3rd Division, 30th Infantry, had gotten used to the monotonous existence of defending what was left of the Anzio beach. Everywhere he looked,

Private First Class John Dutko fired his Browning machine gun from the hip at entrenched German positions. *Congressional Medal of Honor Society.*

the twenty-eight-year-old from Riverside, New Jersey, was surrounded by a honeycomb of wet and muddy trenches, foxholes and dugouts.[162] But the somewhat leisurely, albeit miserable, reprieve from heavy fighting was about to end. At 5:45 a.m. on May 23, 1944, the pre-dawn sky over Anzio, Italy, lit up with explosions of the Allied artillery barrage. The artillery went first, then the armored units, followed closely by the infantry. It was time to seize the roads leading to Rome.

Dutko's Company A's orders to secure a main road junction near Ponte Rotto faltered instantly. Ahead of the men were three heavy German machine gun entrenchments and an 88mm mobile gun position. The family man from New Jersey took his place near other company members in a shallow trench off the side of the road, awaiting a break in the firing—none was forthcoming. Private Anatole J. Simon, who would eventually earn a Bronze Star for his own heroic deeds, looked on at John Dutko clenching his Browning machine gun.[163] The two pairs of eyes met. "I'm going to get that 88 with my heater," shouted the Riverside man, his voice barely audible over the German machine gun fire.[164]

Before Simon could answer, Dutko rose to his full height and, squeezing the trigger of his machine gun as hard as he could, sprang toward the enemy positions. "He must have known he would be killed when he left the cover of the trench; we knew it," the other private recalled. "But he did it anyway."[165]

Dutko ran fast, faster than seemingly possible, for a hundred yards. As the hail of gunfire set on him, the others watching from the trench noticed the Jersey man pull out a grenade and toss it into the nearest machine gun nest. In an instant, the second gun emplacement met its mark, and blood spit out of the back of Dutko's side; he stumbled, fell and then got up again. He jumped into a shell crater, and everyone watching was sure that he would not emerge again.[166] Yet Dutko emerged as quickly as he had entered and, firing his Browning from the hip, raced toward the 88mm cannon emplacement. The enemy bullets kicked up the dirt at his heels, but the private was determined. He stopped ten yards away from the gun emplacement and opened a long burst of fire, killing the five-person crew. Dutko then wheeled around and opened fire at the machine gun nest that had wounded him. The two Germans never had a chance.

There was only one enemy machine gun emplacement left. And although moving much slower and visibly stumbling from the loss of blood, the New Jersey man half ran toward it. The final bullet came swiftly, ripping through his chest. Dutko continued firing his Browning, never stopping his assault forward. While providing covering fire from a nearby position, Simon watched as "the dead man's momentum carried [Dutko] into the last gun nest, where he fell dead on top of the [last two Germans he had just killed]."[167]

The United States 3rd Division suffered 955 casualties that day, in a breakout that would continue until early June and cost many more American lives. The strategic importance of the battle in which Private Dutko gave his life extends past bringing about the liberation of Italy. The two German corps forced to fight at Anzio were initially ordered to move and defend Normandy, where they would have otherwise been on D-Day, thus adding further importance to the Americans' stand in Italy in May 1944. The Allied forces suffered nearly 28,000 casualties during the Battle of Anzio—with the most Congressional Medals of Honor awarded in any single battle of the entire war, at twenty-two.[168] Dutko's Medal of Honor was received by his widow, Mrs. Thel M. Dutko, in October 1944. Most of her friends and family had already learned of her husband's heroic deeds by then. The newspaper headlines back home summarized his last breaths quite literally: "Pvt. John W. Dutko: He Died Killing Nazis."[169]

# TANK WARFARE

There were eight of them—six boys and two girls. Yet in July 1944, it was the four eldest boys who caused Mr. and Mrs. Ben Sadowski the most sleepless nights. They were also the reason the elder couple had four stars on the service flag hanging on their front porch. The Sadowskis' eldest son, John, was just promoted to sergeant with the U.S. Army paratroopers; Michael was a second-class seaman; and their eighteen-year-old, Chester, reported for naval duty the week prior. Their second oldest, Joseph, had just written to them about his promotion from corporal to a technician, fifth grade in the U.S. Army Coast Artillery. The scarier part of the letter for the parents stated that his unit was now making its way across France with the invasion forces.[170]

Sergeant Joseph John Sadowski of Perth Amboy, New Jersey, was a copper plant worker after high school. He enlisted in the U.S. Army in May 1941, before any of his friends and before America's official entrance into the conflict. Joe's Company A, 37th Tank Battalion, 4th Armored Division, under General George S. Patton's 3rd Army, landed at Utah Beach on July 13, 1944, and soon earned the unofficial nickname of the "Breakthrough Division" for its prominent role in moving the armed forces off Normandy. Now, to capitalize on high morale following some key victories across Europe, Allied commanders planned to launch a fast campaign from Normandy to bring the fight closer to the German homeland.[171] Ahead of General Patton's 3rd Army and the Perth Amboy man lay the hilly region of Lorraine, the most direct route toward the German highly fortified western border. On September 5,

1944, after a brief stop caused by fuel shortages, the Americans set off to encircle their first major obstacle on the road to Germany: the French urban center of Nancy.

The life of a M4 Sherman tank crew under the famous George S. Patton was often grimmer than depicted in the newspapers back home. The cramped machines usually carried a crew of five, with a commanding sergeant, a driver, a gunner, a loader and a hull gunner. "Patton was a great pusher, you know," recalled a member of the 3rd Army. "None of that digging holes and staying there…he believed in moving, moving, moving, which we did. Sometimes we would get so far ahead that we were in danger of somebody coming in behind us."[172] Sergeant Sadowski's M4 Sherman tank would often haul infantry on its way through France. "Sometimes ten or twelve men would ride on each vehicle because they couldn't keep up with us lugging around their equipment."[173] Most of these men whom Joe saw were draftees, no older than eighteen or twenty. "The 3rd Armored Division had more children in action than the 101st Airborne," tank gunner Walter Stitt would say.[174] For Sadowski, he was not just the commander of

The M4 Sherman tank was the backbone of the U.S. liberation of Europe. *National World War II Museum.*

his tank crew; he was their leader, their elder who they looked up to, and they were his responsibility.

Sadowski's M4 crew was used to riding into German-occupied towns, but on September 14, 1944, at Valhey, France, as part of the Nancy encirclement, it was different. Typically, the small towns did not cause the 37th Tank Battalion any trouble. "We felt pretty safe inside—especially from small-arms fire," Joe Caserta of the 4th Armored Division stated. "It would just ping off the tank."[175] Another tank gunner recalled, "If someone fired at us from a town with a rifle or whatever, we would put a couple of rounds of high explosives in the roofs of these houses, and that would start a fire… and sometimes burn down the whole town—that often taught them to stop shooting at us."[176] Yet the men knew that anything more prominent, like a German 88 or a Panzerfaust rocket launcher, altered the paradigm. "We did not stand a chance," stated Caserta.

It was late afternoon, and the sun still fighting for its place in the sky when Sadowski's Sherman tank advanced with the lead elements of Combat Command A into Nancy's neighboring town of Valhey. The fire opened up at them from the surrounding structures like a hailstorm. First was small-arms fire, but soon hidden 88mm heavy guns began finding their marks. Sadowski's radio transmitter picked up screams of agony from other tank crews as red fireballs whizzed past his M4. "If the tank got hit, usually somebody was killed," remembered one soldier. "If you saw a tank get hit, you just knew that somebody was going to get it."[177] As Sadowski directed his tank through the intensely severe barrage of enemy fire from the streets and building, it came into the sights of a heavy German gun positioned less than twenty yards away—it would not miss. The Sherman tank jerked violently and burst into flames, filling the small space within with smoke. No one needed to tell the New Jersey sergeant what would come next. "When a tank is stopped in combat, you get the hell out," Caserta would say. "You don't stay near it because they're going to hit it again."[178]

The attack came so suddenly that most of Sadowski's crew hesitated and stayed put, confused and shell-shocked. The Perth Amboy man yelled for his crew to dismount and take cover in the adjoining building. Even before their boots hit the ground, the artillery and machine gun fire zeroed in on the escaping men, chipping at the cobblestones beneath their feet as they ran. A nearby shell explosion threw some of the crew sideways, yet somehow they got up, staggered and continued for cover. The nearby tanks and infantry fired at the enemy positions, with other tanks suffering a similar fate. Sergeant Joe Sadowski dived behind a building corner and began counting the crew members following him—he did not need to recount to know that someone was missing. He looked at his tank, which continued receiving assault from grenades, mortar fire and machine gun nests in the above windows. None of that mattered. Sadowski's bow gunner was still in the tank—unable to open the badly bent bow gunner's hatch.

Sadowski, the leader of the pack, the elder of a bunch of kids, could not stand by and watch. Nobody would ever know what went through his mind as he ran toward the tank through the hail of enemy fire. The New Jersey man managed to get to the tank, mount it and attempt to pry the enflamed gunner's hatch, which burned his hands. He never made it—a machine gun fire stream struck him almost

Joseph J. Sadowski lost his life to enemy fire while returning to a burning M4 Sherman tank to try and rescue one of his crewmen. *Congressional Medal of Honor Society.*

instantly. Following Joe's death, the U.S. government ordered his brothers back stateside, to their parents' great relief. They stood solemnly with the other four siblings, watching Major General Francis B. Mallon present their mother with Joe's Congressional Medal of Honor for his actions of heroism and selfless devotion.[179] One son's ultimate sacrifice was enough for the elderly couple. They found it especially hard to let the remaining Sadowski brothers return for duty, but they did, for perhaps they hoped it would help end the war and bring them all back soon enough.

The New Jersey sergeant's actions inspired those around him to continue their fight for Valhey and nearby Nancy. With the main German position surrounded, the enemy withdrew, allowing Patton's 3rd Army to liberate the town and set up a communication headquarters and the main bridgehead for the rest of the Allied campaign through northern France.[180] Germany awaited.

To those who knew him, Horace Marvin Thorne was simply "Bud" or "Buddy," especially to his friend Lindel Pinson. Always ambitious, after graduating from Middletown High School in 1936, Bud quickly advanced up the corporate ladder at an insurance firm while taking night classes at New York University. Yet, his true passion lay in the outdoors. Having grown up on a farm, Thorne was an avid hunter, fisherman and, most importantly, a horseman. Bud and his three brothers often spent weekends away from home, living outdoors on the Delaware River Gap—a time spent living out his passion, which prompted him to quit his job in March 1941 and enlist in the U.S. Cavalry. There Bud would meet his good friend Lindel and his younger sister, Jessie. For the next two years, the three would develop an enormous bond—one that, in Bud and Jessie's case, would lead to marriage in early 1944, while Bud was serving as a cavalry instructor at Camp Polk, Louisiana.[181]

Bud and Lindel probably recalled their times back home fondly. In three days, it would be their first Christmas away from their loved ones, including Jessie, and their current situation could not get any worse. The Battle of the Bulge had been waging for nearly one week, and the only thing worse than the constant artillery and gunfire was the bitter cold. Axis Sally was there to remind them of their situation every step of the way. A member of the 9th Armored Division serving with Bud recalled the loud German speakers back in the woods that talked to the men crouched in their freezing foxholes. First, they would play some American records, but soon came the "Your wives and girlfriends are probably home in a nice warm building, dancing with some other men. You're over here in the cold." The sultry female voice would say, "There is a big push up North; you might as well give up. The war's over, the German army captured 50,000 Americans and is going all the way to Paris."[182] The men always did their best not to believe her.

When the nine German tank divisions attacked the surprised Americans in the Ardennes forest in mid-December 1944, the weather was some of the worst the U.S. forces had experienced in Europe up to that point. The frigid cold and snowstorms briefly grounded American air cover over the area, veiling the enemy movements and allowing them to push deep into the Allied positions. And it was now the weather that made life miserable for Bud and the other members of the 9th Armored Division. The past week had seen them repel attack after attack to hold back the Germans, while giving hope to the surrounded infantry units ahead of them. "The mornings were bitterly cold and foggy, and the snow was about two feet deep with the fir trees all covered." The relief came every several days, but the rest and regrouping in nearby towns were not much better, as those themselves were always open to German attacks. There was no escaping the misery of battle. By the time it was over in late January, it would claim nineteen thousand American lives, with another seventy thousand wounded.

Combat patrols were a daily part of Bud and Lindel's time in the Ardennes. They would make their way slowly into the unknown, snow-blanketed world, hoping to be just loud enough to not be mistaken as Germans and shot by their colleagues hiding in foxholes. Still, being too loud could welcome an enemy sniper's bullet. As such, some men actually preferred their freezing foxholes to being out in the open. This is where being a part of an armored division had its perks—the patrols were often accompanied by at least one American light tank. The December 21, 1944 patrol was not any different, as Corporal Horace "Bud" Thorne led his men into the heavily wooded area near Grufflingen, Belgium, two light tanks creeping alongside his men. It took a single gunshot to drop one of the American soldiers face-first into fifteen inches of snow, no longer pure white.

As Bud ordered his men to fan out and seek cover, the roar of an engine rose above the melee of gunfire. Apart from infamous German tanks, not much was left that could instill more misery into the terrible survival game at the Battle of the Bulge. As the huge Mark III launched forward from seemingly nowhere, the American tanks wasted little time in firing their guns. And although the Panzer-class tank could no longer move, its turret and machine gun continued the fight. Bud and his men had stumbled on a heavily entrenched German position, with an enemy machine gun and anti-tank Panzerfaust fire quickly doing away with their light tank cover. The men were on their own. And if they had any chance of survival, the crippled Mark III needed silencing. Bud's first shots killed the two exposed tank crew members, but the large smoking machine continued firing. Sergeant Pinson later wrote that he knew what his best friend and brother-in-law was going to do—one could see it in Thorne's face.[183] The two men's eyes locked; Bud nodded and left the cover of a nearby tree toward the machine gun fire. Lindel fired his rifle past his friend's head in his best attempt to cover Bud's low advance toward the broken German tank.

The New Jersey man crept as close as possible to the Mark III, searching his belt for two grenades. He removed the pins and threw the explosives into the tank's open turret. With the remaining men inside dead, the Panzer-class tank finally fell silent. Still, the broken machine looked menacing as bullets pinged off its shell from every direction. It might have been when Bud saw the opportunity of the tank's favorable position right at the edge of the enemy line. Making a stand this close to the Germans gave one a direct line of fire at the enemy machine gun nests. Thorne half crawled and half ran back to his original position, where he secured his Browning machine gun. Lindel yelled back at him not to go, but Bud did not hear him.

Dragging the gun and ammo behind him, Thorne made it to the safety of the broken-down tank. To the astonishment of those around him, Bud climbed the top of the tank and, having brought his machine gun,

# Nation Honors Thorne At Ceremonies Today

NEW MONMOUTH.—The Congressional Medal of Honor, the nation's highest decoration, will be awarded posthumously today to Corp. Horace Marvin Thorne, the first Monmouth county man ever to receive it and the fifth recipient from New Jersey. Brig. Gen. Stephen H. Sherrill, commanding general of the Eastern Signal Corps Training center, will make the award to the hero's wife, Mrs. Leah Thorne of DeSoto, Mo.

Corporal Thorne was killed by German fire in Belgium last December, four days before Christmas. The citation accompanying the award states that he was the leader of a combat patrol in the 89th Cavalry divison, which was assigned to the task of driving German forces from dug-in positions in a heavily wooded area. When a German tank stalled nearby Thorne killed its occupants and at the risk of his life inched forward alone thru intense machine

(See THORNE Page 6)

CORP. HORACE M. THORNE

"Bud" Thorne set up a machine gun position on top of a broken-down tank and held off a German advance. *From the* Asbury Park Evening Press.

laid down on the back of the vehicle's rear deck. The first burst of Bud's machine gun fire surprised and disoriented the Germans, as it appeared that their tank was firing at them. The platoon's men took advantage and moved closer to the enemy position, intensifying their fire. From the top of the tank, exposed to enemy fire but laying as prone as he could, Corporal Thorne sent volley after volley of bullets at the Germans. Lindel watched his friend single-handedly dispose of two machine gun nests, killing eight enemy soldiers. When Bud reloaded and turned his gun on an additional machine gun emplacement, the Americans watched its crew abandon its position and retreat deeper into the woods.

As ferociously and abruptly as Bud's machine gun began firing, it now stopped dead in its tracks. "Come back, Bud! Come back!" Lindel yelled as he quickly dodged behind a tree as bullets ripped through the bark where his face had been just a moment before.[184] Back at the tank, the twenty-six-year-old Bud realized that his weapon had jammed and had started fixing it when a lone enemy soldier ran toward the tank and shot him from close range. Lindel managed to free himself from behind the tree and run toward the Mark III tank, already knowing what he would find there. He would tell his sister and Bud's parents that he was "certain that [Bud] was fully aware of the extreme danger of his position when he advanced into enemy territory alone."[185] That is just the type of man that Horace "Bud" Thorne was.

The Congressional Medal of Honor was presented to Bud's wife and his parents in New Jersey on November 17, 1945. Bud's room and personal belongings at his parents' farm in Middletown were "just as he left them," his mother would say. She recalled how a crow her son once trained to tap on his window, and which had not been around since Thorne's enlistment, returned to its perch outside Bud's room and sat quietly, as if waiting in the days following the telegram that informed them of their son's death.[186]

Lindel finished up his tour of duty, surviving the Battle of the Bulge, where the American 3rd Army held on until the weather cleared just three days after Bud gave his life. With the open skies, five thousand Allied aircraft struck at German supply columns and isolated the battlefield.[187] The "Bulge" was eliminated within three weeks, and the Germans were in full retreat. At a small distance from where the Mark III tank once stood in Grufflingen, Belgium, on which Bud Thorne made his last stand, there now stands a stone marker bearing his name and telling his story. Horace "Bud" Thorne's body returned home to Middletown and was buried at a local cemetery. The hero's Medal of Honor is on display in a school named in his honor, the Thorne Middle School, in Middletown, New Jersey, reminding local children each day of the importance of selflessness, character and initiative.

# BEFORE THE END

The American journalist for the Hearst Company, William L. Shirer, arrived in Nuremberg, Germany, just a few days before the September 5, 1934, opening day ceremonies for the 6th Nazi Party Congress. He now stood in awe among the 700,000 loyal supporters meeting in the medieval city—the seat of power for German kings now turned nexus of the Nazi party and ideology. For years, the world watched images of Adolf Hitler's poisonous, racist, ultra-nationalistic and overly militaristic annual Nuremberg Party rallies. While Berlin was the undisputed capital of Germany, the city of Nuremberg acted as the fulcrum of Hitler's National Socialist Workers Party and the Third Reich.

The opening ceremony was held inside a large hall, the Kulturevereins Haus, within the center of the grand city, characterized by beautiful old Gothic architecture buildings mixed with recent Nazi additions of Neoclassical style. The yearly rallies saw hundreds of thousands of men and women parade through the very heart of Nuremberg, the Alter Stadt (the Old Town), past Nuremberg City Hall and through Hauptmarkt Main Square, now renamed Adolf Hitler Platz.[188] Shirer marveled at the area's beauty when walking the city the previous evening, yet the dark symbolism of the event he was there to see was not lost on him. The American journalist stopped walking when he came across a mass of ten thousand men and women outside Hitler's hotel. "We want our Fuhrer!" they all shouted in unison. "I was a little shocked at their faces," Shirer wrote. "When Hitler finally appeared on the balcony for a moment…[around me] I saw crazed

Thousands of Nazi troops listened to a speech by Adolf Hitler in Nuremberg. *Associated Press.*

expressions…they looked up at him as if he were a Messiah, their faces transformed into something positively inhuman."[189]

He now stood with the thousands of other attendees at the opening ceremony, pencil and notebook in hand, awaiting the Nazi leader. The hall around him was a sea of vivid red, black and white Nazi flags everywhere he turned. And then the band stopped playing, and a hush came over the thirty thousand people who packed the hall.[190] Thousands of hands quietly raised in salute as Hitler, Goring, Goebbels, Hess and Himmler slowly walked down the long center aisle. Hitler walked up to the podium, looked around him and began: "The German form of life is determined for the next thousand years!"[191] The crowd erupted in cheers.

FIRST LIEUTENANT FRANCIS XAVIER Burke moved slowly ahead of Company D riflemen through the ruins of Nuremberg, Germany. The 3rd Infantry Division had fought its way into the city that Tuesday morning, April 17, 1945. Now, everywhere Burke looked, the beautiful town was no more—just piles of rubble and ruin. Nuremberg was severely damaged in the Allied strategic bombings that began in 1943. Most recently, on January 2, 1945, the city was so systematically bombed that about 90 percent of it was destroyed in only one hour, with an estimated 1,800 residents killed and roughly 100,000 displaced.[192] The Jersey City man advanced forward as the battalion transportation officer, selecting a motor-pool site. Only by the time he came upon ten Germans making preparations for a local counterattack within the ruins of an abandoned building did he realize that he was a bit too far ahead of the rest of the group.

Frank Burke was born in New York City's infamous Hell's Kitchen neighborhood. Afraid of their children's safety, Frank's parents moved the family across the Hudson River to Jersey City, New Jersey, when he was still a child.[193] His interest in the military led him to enlist in the New Jersey Army National Guard before the start of the Second World War, which placed Frank right in line to be called up for active duty as the nation entered the conflict in 1941; he was twenty-three years old. Before he found himself in the heart of the Nazi cultural center in Nuremberg, Germany, Burke had survived most of the major theaters of war in Europe. Part of the U.S. Army's 1st Battalion, 15th Regiment, 3rd Infantry, the Jersey City man served with distinction in North Africa, in the Battle of Anzio of the Italian campaign and finally in France and the final push into Germany. As he now made his way through the ruins of the old German City, even Frank did not doubt that the thousand-year Reich was at its end. Hitler only had thirteen days to live, and Victory in Europe Day was less than three weeks away. Still, because of the city's symbolism, taking Nuremberg was essential to breaking German morale.

By the time Burke's U.S. 3rd Infantry Division entered the city that morning, Heinrich Himmler had issued orders that any male occupant, regardless of age, who showed any inkling of surrendering was to be immediately shot.[194] Armed with whatever weapons were left and identified by simple armbands, the local citizens prepared themselves for the imminent onslaught of the American military might—some as young as twelve. Three hanged bodies swayed in the wind above Burke as he quietly made his way forward. The makeshift poster near the dead men read in German, "Cowardly, selfish, and disloyal traitors."[195] This was what the war had become—the fight the young New Jersey man and his fellow soldiers were entering was one where surrendering was not an option.

Francis X. Burke earned his Medal of Honor in the last weeks of the war in Europe while fighting Germany's last-ditch effort in the streets of war-torn Nuremberg, Germany. *Congressional Medal of Honor Society.*

Apart from the radicalized Hitler's Youth and local resistance, the three German battle groups tasked with defending the city were willing to do anything to ensure that the Americans did not secure Nuremberg. Unbeknownst to the 3rd Infantry Division, the men were now entering into one giant time bomb, as the SS rigged entire neighborhoods to explode lest they fall into enemy hands. It was taking the American forces hours to clear the city blocks. Nearly all house windows acted as sniper or Panzerfaust nests, while bomb craters on every street were used to camouflage machine gun posts.[196]

The immediate silence around Burke almost drowned out the sound of small gunfire in the distance as he made his way up the street. The American units had entered the city from numerous locations, and the fighting was fierce all around the city. The first lieutenant passed a body of a dead German soldier on his right yet continued undeterred—the men knew that sometimes even stepping near one might set off the rigged booby traps the Germans left on them. Burke looked toward a building in his sights and noticed a group of German men preparing for an attack. Realizing that they had not seen the lone American soldier, who had gotten too ahead of his scouting party, Burke quietly retreated toward his unit and asked for a Thompson machine gun. He informed his men of the German position and then asked for covering fire as he hunched over his body and trotted toward the opening in the building wall, presumably caused by an American bombing run, and where now the Germans awaited.

This time, Frank was not so lucky. His eyes had barely met those of the enemy soldier when he was forced to squeeze his trigger and stop the German mid-warning yell. Single shots, machine gun fire and grenades shot out from the German position toward the Jersey City man. Burke fired his light machine gun as he jumped behind concrete debris in the middle of the street. To his left, another enemy machine gun emplacement he had previously not seen began firing. Burke turned quickly and shot his attacker, exhausting the ammunition in his clip. Just as he reloaded his weapon, some of the German soldiers from the original position moved closer to dislodge him from his relative safety. Burke managed to kill the advancing enemy soldiers by firing blindly above the rubble. It might have been at that moment that he realized the firefight was all around him and that this was not a single-man fight. American troops whizzed past him, running from building to building, cover to cover, while returning fire from the often fanatical German soldiers. Finally out of machine gun ammo, the first lieutenant reached out for an M1 Garand rifle lying near a dead soldier who would never need it again.

Rifle in hand, Burke ran about one hundred yards, lifting his feet as high as he could and making giant strides to avoid the shower of bullets ricocheting all around him. He had hardly slid behind an abandoned tank before a bullet pinged off its metal hull an inch away from his face. Burke looked down to a cellar window directly across the street, twenty yards away. The sniper was reloading when the New Jersey man ran toward the low window, rapidly firing his rifle. The M1 ammo clip pinged away from the rifle with its infamous loud noise that would often spell doom for the American infantryman by notifying the enemy that he was out of ammo. But it did not matter here. As the tall man crashed into the dark basement through the small window, the German sniper lay dead on the ground. Burke watched him as he reloaded his rifle with his last bloc clip—eight rounds was not enough.

Crawling out of the basement and back into the fight, Burke collected any spare ammunition from other company members and secured hand grenades as he ran from cover to cover. Gunfire from nearby ruins finally pinned him down. The lieutenant stayed low behind a corner of a building, firing toward the adjacent structure. Seeing his ammo dwindle and being without many prospects for getting out of the situation, Burke put down his M1 and pulled the pins from two grenades. He took a deep breath and, without giving the enemy much chance, launched himself into the ruins of the enemy building. His two explosives reached the Germans at the same time their single potato masher grenade landed by Burke's feet—the triple

Burke's 3rd Infantry Division in the Battle of Nuremberg. *National Archives.*

explosion threw some men into the corners of the three-walled room and some into the street.

Burke awoke almost instantly, lying on the ground among a shower of debris and what was once the building's top floor, now scattered all around him. Staggering to the street, the first lieutenant retraced his steps to where he had left his rifle. Still dazed, with his ears ringing and his face covered in dust and sweat, the young man picked up his M1 Garand right in time to swing around and fire three shots at the pistol-wielding German man who had followed him. Burke reloaded his rifle and exited the building. He then followed the popping sound of gunfire to make his way toward the fighting, reaching his platoon amid a vicious firefight with an enemy stronghold. For the next thirty minutes, the New Jersey man fought bitterly against entrenched Germans only to move down the street to do it all over again.

With each hour and each street block, the resistance dwindled. American trucks with large speakers followed the soldiers into the streets, bellowing in German. "Your city is completely surrounded, and the old city has been entered in several places. Your unconditional surrender will be accepted... [and] you will be treated humanely," said the stern voice carrying far and wide through Nuremberg. Burke and his fellow soldiers continued clearing the streets as the voice around them proclaimed, "Raise white flags over the buildings and open all entrances to the inner city. Otherwise, you will be destroyed. We will not wait, so act quickly."[197] Yet the thinly veiled 20mm German gun Burke and his men just came upon continued to fire in their direction. Working together with other soldiers, Burke flanked the position and shot what would prove to be some of the last resistance troops that Nuremberg could muster that day. He did not know how many enemy soldiers he had killed. Still, later estimates would point to eleven confirmed and an additional twenty-nine possible—anything to help him and his men survive that day.[198]

The struggle for Nuremberg finally ended three days later, on April 20, 1945, Hitler's birthday. Instead of fanatical Nazi attacks anticipated by Burke and other troops of the 3rd Infantry because of the occasion, the Germans instead chose to lay down their weapons. Apart from one enemy attack in one section of the city in the early dawn, all was quiet. Lieutenant Francis Xavier Burke found himself standing among other American soldiers in the shadow of a large, now ruined church inside the Hauptmarkt Main Square, also known as Adolf Hitler Platz. It was once full of joyous Nazis; now it was an empty ghost square. It was a memory he would occasionally return to years later when marching in parades and speaking with high school students about his time overseas.[199] The humble man would always choose to talk about the end of the war more so than his actions during it. Nor would he spend too much time discussing that April 1945 day that would earn him the ticket to Washington, D.C., to meet the president of the United States on January 9, 1946. "His extraordinary bravery and superb fighting skill," the Congressional Medal of Honor citation would go on to read, "were an inspiration to his comrades, and his voluntary mission into extremely dangerous territory hastened the fall of Nuremberg, in his battalion's sector."[200]

The war might not have been over when Burke and his fellow soldiers stood in Hauptmarkt Square, but there was little doubt among them that the world would not live to see the thousand-year Reich. A few blocks away, the large stadium where hundreds of thousands of Nazi supporters once shouted Hitler's name stood quiet, the field pockmarked with large bomb craters, hundreds of half-torn swastika flags lining up the destroyed ruins. Before moving on from Nuremberg, the Americans destroyed the last specter of the Nazi nightmare by detonating the stadium's twenty-foot-tall swastika.[201] Now that, Burke would likely say, was a sight worth remembering.

Francis X. Burke returned stateside to his wife, Catherine, with whom he would have four children. The two lived happily until Frank's death on September 6, 1988, at sixty-nine. Burke was buried at Brigadier General William C. Doyle Veterans Memorial Cemetery in Wrightstown, New Jersey.[202]

# OKINAWA

The pre-war U.S. Armed Forces' Guide to the Pacific briefed visitors to the Ryukyus, of which Okinawa is the main island, with the following: "Those who wish a good memento of a stay in Nansei Shoto should get a piece of lacquerware for which the islanders are famous." In the words of historian Max Hastings, "in the spring of 1945, some 12,000 Americans and up to 150,000 Japanese found death rather than porcelain amid Okinawa's sixty-mile length of fields and mountains, or in the waters offshore."[203] By the time the Battle of Okinawa ended on June 22, 1945, two New Jersey men's actions would earn them the Congressional Medal of Honor—one would never make it home to share it with his family.

The American "Island Hopping" strategy to retake the Pacific from the imperial forces of Japan was nearing its end. What began in 1942 with the invasion of Guadalcanal, 3,000 miles away from Tokyo, had by 1944 brought the Americans to Iwo Jima and closed the distance to 750 miles—Okinawa, the southernmost island of Japan, would be half that.[204] The one thing that nobody needed to explain to the twenty-three-year-old Martin O. May and twenty-nine-year-old John W. Meagher, who fought with the 307th and 305th Infantries, respectively, was that the closer their units got to Japan, the more brutal the fighting would become.

Born and raised in Phillipsburg, New Jersey, May was barely a year out of high school when he joined the army, which saw him assigned to the 305th Infantry Regiment of the 77th Infantry Division. John Meagher, May's older compatriot and another soon-to-be Medal of Honor recipient, was drafted

American battleship sending rockets at shores of Okinawa, five days before the invasion. *Library of Congress.*

into the U.S. Army out of Jersey City in March 1942 and moved to the 307th. The two men never knew each other. Yet by the time their 77th Division landed on Okinawa, which apart from the Normandy invasion of 1944 was the largest amphibious war operation, May and Meagher had already seen action in Guam and Leyte. And as bad as that was, Okinawa would be even worse.

The first week of April 1945 witnessed more than 1,200 vessels transporting 180,000 U.S. soldiers and marines to an island characterized by farmland and high hills and populated by 450,000 people and an additional 100,000 Japanese warriors.[205] A Marine Corps private later wrote, "We were resigned only to the fact that the Japanese would fight to total extinction on Okinawa." This operation was no longer about island-hopping toward Japan—this *was* Japan. And the enemy would do anything to protect it.

Using extensive propaganda, the Japanese empire convinced its force, both the regular army and the Okinawa locals, to fight to the death. The island's men and women were conscripted as guerrillas, and home guard units had been told that the Americans would rape, torture and murder them and that it was quicker and more honorable to take their own lives instead of surrendering.[206] "We gave them all some candy, but they still refused to touch it unless one of us ate some of it first. You could tell they didn't trust us as far as they could throw us," recalled a member of Private May's unit.[207] Witnessing suicides on Okinawa was as normal as the carnage of battle, images many veterans would carry with them for the rest of their lives. It was one thing to fight against a formidable and determined foe and quite another to fight against one unafraid of death.

Okinawa Island, the biggest of the Ryukyu Islands at the southernmost point of the Japanese island chain, presented a formidable challenge for the members of the 77th Division tasked with taking its southern elevation. Knowing that its naval power was no match for the Japanese, the enemy commanders allowed the American forces to land a foothold near the centrally located western shore of the island. With weak opposition, the 100,000 army soldiers and 80,000 marines quickly gained the island's fulcrum. Part of the army's infantry, the New Jersey men were tasked with continuing Okinawa's takeover by working southward, while the marines took the northern route. The Japanese strategy called for using the many hills, ridges and ravines on the island's extremities to pin down U.S. units in a war of attrition using guerrilla and ambush tactics.

The torrential downpours, nonexistent in the first days of the landings, now seemed to coincide with the ferocious fighting that began once the army moved to secure the remainder of the island. The open farm fields became a turkey shoot for Japanese artillery, while the harsher terrain swallowed up young men at unprecedented speeds. Ridge by ridge and through small gaps in terrain, which forced the American units to attack in lesser numbers, the Japanese inflicted damage previously unseen by Private First Class Martin O. May and his fellow soldiers. The rain only worsened things, especially for the army, which relied heavily on motorized warfare. "It was the most ghastly corner of hell I had ever witnessed," wrote one soldier. "As far as I could see, an area that previously had been a low grassy valley with a picturesque stream meandering through it was a muddy, repulsive, open sore on the land. Every crater was half full of water, and many of them held an American corpse; with bodies laying pathetically just as they had been killed, half submerged in muck and water, rusting weapons still in hand."[208]

Private May, like his counterparts, spent many days wearing a drenched poncho—braving through sloppy mud terrain, wet and collapsing foxholes and slick mountain ranges. The artillery-induced headaches were getting to him, yet he continued. Around him, the foul smell of decomposing corpses was spread by the warm subtropical wind.[209] "Many a man had slipped in the mud," said one soldier, "finding himself covered in maggots, face to face with a half-buried, decomposing Japanese or American soldier.[210] This was Martin's war when he climbed up on a ridge looking for an advantageous machine gun position on April 19, 1945—one he would never come down from alive.

The rugged slopes of Ie-Shima adequately represented the difficult Okinawa terrain the Americans were tasked with conquering. As with previous actions, the Japanese waited for infantry to move into a tight geographical position in a low valley before unleashing artillery and machine

Private First Class Martin O. May blasted fanatical Japanese troops on Okinawa with hand grenades until he was mortally wounded. *Congressional Medal of Honor Society.*

gun fire. Every crevice and every jagged edge above housed enemy fire that picked off May's company one by one. The young New Jerseyan scanned the hillside and found what he sought: a high point just low enough for him to climb. Dragging his heavy machine gun, May made his way up the ridge, returning down multiple times to bring up additional ammunition. Disregarding his safety, with bullets and explosions throwing pieces of rock into the air around him, the private set up his makeshift machine gun nest, found his first target and began what would turn into a three-day stand.

The Japanese soldiers did not take too long to notice the lone soldier assaulting them with accurate bursts from above. And neither did the American rifle company below, which took advantage of the situation to press on the attack and gain favorable defensive positions by getting out of the open ravine. It also helped that Private May became the primary target for the enemy's artillery and small gunfire, allowing the men below to take their time with more accurate shots. Still, the more men they killed, the more Japanese troops arrived to reinforce them. Up above on the ridge, Private May found himself losing sight of what he was firing at as explosions and ricocheting bullets threw blinding dust and dirt about him. The Jersey man let his finger off the trigger and peeked down below. The mist cleared to show a group of advancing enemy soldiers ready to scale his position. Martin removed the pin from a grenade on his belt without thinking and threw it toward the men. It took an additional two to stifle the charge against him.

The enemy temporarily suspended forward attacks but kept the Americans at bay with artillery for the remainder of the night. When someone finally made it up to his perch and asked Martin to come down and rest, Private May refused and instead asked for water and additional ammo. Stray machine gun bursts continued ringing throughout the night as the occasional artillery shell lit up the sky and shook the ground. All around lay the silent and the unseen, the Americans and Japanese equally awaiting the dawn to resume the killing and the dying. High in his makeshift machine gun nest sat a New Jersey boy who had turned twenty-three years old just the day before. Likely the soldiers did not know that, nor would May care to come down and tell them. Perhaps he would say something when the day was over and he got down from his ridge, and they could all laugh at the craziness of war.

As expected, the enemy renewed its attack early on April 21, 1945, and Private First Class Martin O. May was ready. The Japanese seemed even more determined to knock the New Jersey man out of his advantageous position. For the next few hours, the enemy's devastating rifle, machine gun and mortar fire pummeled May's position—all to no avail. While the American casualties mounted in the ravine below, the private continued to fire his machine gun. A mortar finally met its mark and threw the young man backward. Although severely wounded and bleeding from multiple lacerations, May crawled back to his gun only to find that the explosion had destroyed it. Still undeterred, Martin moved closer to the edge and lined up all the grenades he had on him. For a while, the private managed to blast unrelenting Japanese troops with his hand grenades, failing to notice an enemy soldier on the nearby ridge aiming his rifle. Death came swiftly for Private Martin O. May—the hero of Okinawa, who managed to hold the American line, largely by himself and despite unmeasurable odds.

JOHN W. MEAGHER, THE twenty-nine-year-old Jersey City man, stood before the Hudson County honorary judge and awaited his swearing-in as the new court attendant. It had been a year since the war ended, and Meagher returned home to his lovely wife, Ann, and his pre-war job as a railroad checker. And although he was very excited about this new job, he could really do without the fanfare and the press present at the occasion. After numerous individuals spoke about the honor of having a Congressional Medal of Honor recipient work for the county, it was John's turn to speak. The newspapers called it the shortest speech on record at the courthouse. The tall, lanky man stood up, walked to the front of the room and said, "Self-praise stinks," before returning to his seat.[211] Those who knew him as Sergeant John William Meagher would not have blinked an eye.

It had been two months since the death of President Franklin D. Roosevelt and more than a month since Victory in Europe Day, yet there he was, riding on top of a Sherman tank along with other members of Company E, 305th Infantry Regiment, 77th Infantry Division. The war in the Pacific dragged on. Meagher arrived on Okinawa in March 1945, partaking in the advance into the island's southernmost point along with the 77th Division. It was now June 19, and the island was nearly all secure, yet that did not mean the enemy was any less determined or fanatical in their defense of the island.

U.S. marines advancing through the ridges of Okinawa. *National World War II Museum.*

And even though Okinawa's commanders would surrender to the Americans in three days, neither John nor the Japanese troops hiding in the nearby cave positions Company E were tasked with clearing out knew any of that. On that Tuesday, surrender was not an option, especially for the Japanese, many of whom still believed that "young American men qualified for the Army by murdering their parents, and routinely raped and killed women in Asia."[212] A young island local would remember those last days on Okinawa: "We were simply given hand grenades and told not to throw them until we could see the whites of the Americans' eyes."[213] Sergeant Meagher must have felt the tank's rumble beneath him as he scanned the nearby ravines for movement—the quiet before the storm. But then the troops moved deeper into the gorge, and bullets splattered about them.

Instead of jumping off the Sherman, John directed the turret machine gunner and the main gunner inside toward the fortified targets, calling them out as they appeared. The bullets pinged off the shell and bounced all around him as the sergeant fired his semi-automatic M1 Garand rifle while continuing to provide directions. With the firefight all around them, the New Jersey man caught movement in the corner of his eye and snapped his head to see a lone Japanese soldier running toward the tank holding a grenade. Meagher jumped off the tank just in time, springing at the attacker with his bayonet extended. The two men had not even hit the ground when the enemy's grenade exploded, killing the Japanese soldier instantly and throwing the sergeant unconscious to the ground.

Perhaps to his surprise, John opened his eyes a few moments later and patted down his body to ensure that it was all there. And then the sound of war returned, the firefight still alive ahead of him with men firing and returning fire. Meagher reached for his rifle lying near him only to find that it was torn apart by the blast. The Sherman tank he had been riding stood silently a few feet away. There was no time to think. The New Jerseyan got up and, keeping his head down as bullets whizzed past it, made his way toward the tank, climbing up to its turret and the .50-caliber M2 Browning machine gun. He first tried kicking the pintle lock with his foot to dislodge the heavy machine gun from the gun pedestal, but he found more luck with the mounting pins closer to the trigger. The weapon felt heavy, and the long ammo belt forced him to wrap it around his other arm.

The army would call his action "a furious one-man assault on the enemy."[214] Meagher jumped down from the tank and ran toward the fight. The heavy machine gun on his hip pushed him back just a little with each squeeze of the trigger, his arms using all their strength to control its onslaught. Firing from his hip and moving through vicious crossfire that ripped through his clothing, John charged the nearest pillbox.[215] The M2 Browning tore through the six enemy soldiers in an instant. The Japanese had by then become aware of the new danger and concentrated their hand grenades and machine gun fire on the New Jersey man. Going on amid the hail of bullets and explosions, John dashed for the second enemy gun. He made it just as his Browning ran out of ammunition. Without much thought, the sergeant grabbed the Browning by the handle and barrel. It felt hot on his hand, but anything else would surely mean death. Meagher stormed the pillbox swinging the heavy machine gun like a baseball bat. By the time he was done, no one was left to oppose him.

The fighting continued around him, but it looked all but over by the time the New Jersey man emerged from the enemy machine gun nest and let the M2 drop to his feet. Congress would award twenty-three Medals of Honor during the entire Okinawa campaign. John W. Meagher's action of June 19, just forty-eight hours before the Japanese surrender, would be the last one to be awarded the prestigious decoration. Unlike many of his brothers in arms who also placed the lives of others ahead of their own, the New Jersey man lived to tell the tale, returning home to Jersey City in 1946. And while he hardly ever spoke about the incident, it did not stop others from praising his service. John died peacefully surrounded by his family on April 14, 1996, at seventy-eight. He is buried at Arlington National Cemetery.

John Meagher and his wife, Ann, read a congratulatory message at their home notifying them that John will be receiving the Medal of Honor. *From the* Paterson Evening News, *1946.*

The Battle of Okinawa proved to be the main deterrent from launching a full-scale invasion of mainland Japan and one of the main reasons used to justify dropping the atomic bombs on Hiroshima and Nagasaki less than two months later. Ironically, the island that led to the end of America's involvement in one major war would be the assembly point for two others. From 1945 to 1972, the U.S. government administered Okinawa, twenty years longer than the Allied occupation of Japan following the Second World War.[216] It would use the island as a staging ground for the Korean War in the early 1950s and the Vietnam War less than a decade later. By then, many people had moved on and forgotten about the horrors of Okinawa and World War II. Those worries would soon return with a new Cold War conflict with the Soviet Union and its various proxy wars that brought Americans to far-off places such as Korea and Vietnam. The latter was a new type of conflict that the American people had a much tougher time getting behind, leaving many young men who fought in it feeling abandoned by their fellow countrymen.

# PART IV

---

# KOREA AND VIETNAM

---

*Sometimes you will find yourself in the wrong place at the wrong time—deal with it the best you can.*

*—Don Jenkins, Medal of Honor recipient*

# ONE OF THE CHOSIN FEW

The lanky Hector Albert Cafferata Jr. of Montville, New Jersey, stood quietly in the sun-bathed rose garden of the White House. The army, navy and marine brass stood around him, watching President Harry S Truman fasten the Congressional Medal of Honor around his neck. Hector looked ahead past the officials and found his parents, brothers, relatives and the beautiful Dolores, soon to be his wife. He nodded. Monday, November 24, 1952, was much different from the November day two years ago that brought him to this moment, starting with the sun now gently heating his face.

The shy young man from Montville stood silently as President Truman read the citation that accompanied his medal "almost as though he had begun to doubt that he had done all the things he was being lauded for."[217] The president then turned and spoke to him, but when asked about it later, all Cafferata could say was, "I can't remember what he told me."[218] Truman shook the twenty-three-year-old's hand, and everyone turned toward the group of journalists. An Associated Press photographer called out, "Smile buddy, so we can get a good picture!" The former private first class, the holder of the nation's highest award for valor, looked blankly ahead with a sad expression. "I am sorry, I can't smile."[219]

THE END OF THE Korean conflict, more commonly referred to as the Korean War, seemed all but assured in November 1950. The United States–led

United Nations forces, supported by military units from the Republic of Korea, had pushed the invading North Korean People's Army back past the 49th parallel. American general Douglas MacArthur's rapid advance up the Korean Peninsula brought some units, specifically the X Corps, up to the Yalu River, which separated Korea from Communist China. As the temperatures in the northernmost mountains of Korea dropped, the generals continued pushing their men to advance farther. By late November, the 1st Marine Division, with Hector Cafferata Jr. of the 7th Marines, 2nd Battalion, Company F, and some units of the 7th Infantry Division, took up positions in the snowcapped mountains around Chosin Reservoir.[220] The assurances of the war ending by Christmas poured in from MacArthur's headquarters in Tokyo, Japan, but the situation on the ground near Chosin was about to go from bad to worse. Thousands of Chinese troops waited behind the Yalu on the other side of the frigid mountains, where the New Jerseyan and his fellow soldiers were already deep in battle with the unforgiving winter.

Private Cafferata came to Korea in October after training at Camp Pendleton in California—the first thing he would recall remembering was the bitter cold, especially after having arrived from the sunny West Coast. The Boonton High School graduate and all-star football player back home came near the Yalu River on the Chosin Reservoir just as a Siberian cold front descended on the region, plunging the temperatures down as low as thirty-six degrees below zero. James Brady, a marine platoon leader, would later write in his memoir of the time spent in the cold mountains of Korea when the snow buried the land. "The peaks and the valleys and everything but the closest apron of wire, the nearest bunker, the yellowed ammo-tube urinal stuck in the snow, everything but those and the war itself were blotted out."[221]

The soldiers' light clothes and general-issue uniforms left a lot to be desired. Then an unfounded rumor rendered newly sent warmer jackets lined with fiberglass useless. News spread that if one got shot through them, the bullet would carry tiny fragments of glass into the body. "And because the fragments were glass and not metal, the aid stations and even the hospital ship could not trace them inside you, and you'd never get rid of the slivers. They would cut and tear at you and work into your intestines and cause infections and hemorrhaging the rest of your life," Brady said, recalling the gist of the rumor. So Private Cafferata and others from the 1st Marine Division continued fighting their war against winter. "The wind would come up at forty miles an hour and blow that snow up," wrote another member of the 2nd Battalion, 7th Marines. "The snow would sting you. The

A group of marines taking a break near the Chosin Reservoir. *Associated Press.*

weapons wouldn't fire [because] they would freeze." Even putting up shelter proved a daunting task. "The ground was so cold that if we wanted to put up a shelter half, we would put a stick upright on the ground and pee on it."[222] Hands and feet froze almost at will, as did all weapons, batteries and soon, the worse of them all, morphine and all other medical supplies. It seemed that the New Jersey man would have been lucky to survive the snow-capped mountains, but the Chinese army had other plans for the Americans instead of letting them simply freeze to death.

Cafferata's unit was charged with protecting a section of the seventy-eight-mile road connecting Hungnam and the Chosin Reservoir—the area's major highway cut out of Korea's hilly terrain and large peaks and characterized by steep climbs and sudden drops. On the other side of the mountain, the 120,000-man Chinese army was finally ready to carry out Chairman Mao Zedong's orders to annihilate the American force near the Chosin. A few minutes after midnight on November 27, 1950, Cafferata heard strange sounds from the woods below Company F's position. Cymbals clanged and bugles blared as loudspeakers belted out in broken English, "Marines, tonight you die!"[223] The marines ripped off their sleeping bags and jumped for their weapons. The sentries strained their eyes to see the slopes below them seemingly moving—swarming with thousands of white quilted uniforms coming to overwhelm them. Star shells burst above, illuminating the scary sight below. The lead marine elements held their positions with machine guns, grenades and M1 Garand rifles, but it was no match for the sheer number of Chinese troops running through their lines. Fighting soon broke into hand-to-hand combat along the entire line—bending but not breaking.

A marine would later marvel at the neatness of men dying in winter in his memoirs of the first moments of the Chinese attack. "All winter, you were so muffed in clothes, layers, and layers, swaddled against the cold, that a man could be all shot to pieces, literally sieved, but unless you were a corpsman, you didn't have to look at the broken bones and the torn flesh and see blood pulsating from cut arteries and veins."[224] Dead men soon covered the two peeks near the reservoir's Toktong pass section of the highway, where the young Cafferata fired his M1, probably forgetting the number of times he had reloaded his rifle in just the first twenty minutes of fighting. Medics rushed from man to man, holding syringes with morphine in their mouths to best thaw them and make them usable on the crying young men. They cursed the frozen bags of plasma now rendered useless but so very needed.

The private from New Jersey found himself shooting in different directions, the most distressing being the one behind him. His company's section of the line was breaking, but even worse was the silence from the American position around him. Bodies littered the ground, limbs sticking up against the otherwise dark sky. "Some Marines, they froze solid the way they died," recalled another veteran. "You had to break some arms to get them in body bags; it was terrible."[225] Ahead of Cafferata, the trip wires with grenades hanging from them that he and his men put up the day before were doing the trick. Like some formations around him, Hector's sector was cut off, surrounded and, worse yet, about to be overrun. The Dover, Morris County man maneuvered up and down the line, delivering accurate fire at onrushing Chinese. With each pass, he would bend down to pick up additional ammo for his rifle and grenades from his fallen comrades—quickly dispensing all, only to restock on another pass. Sometimes he would hand an empty M1 to the wounded men who lay near him, who would then return it to him reloaded—often, they did not live the extra second to see Cafferata fire it.

He was unsure how long he was up there holding the line, but Hector knew that he was alone. For hours, armed with only grenades and a rifle and wearing only socks and a light jacket he managed to grab as he leaped out of his sleeping bag, the New Jersey man fought off waves of incoming enemy soldiers.[226] With the dawn upon him, the private finally heard American artillery and machine gun fire coming closer to his position from the rear. The reinforcements filled the shallow entrenchment that Cafferata had called home for the last few hours; unfazed, he continued his stand. Hector was still picking off advancing troops when he heard the grenade land among a group of wounded marines.

Turning quickly, Hector launched toward the explosive on the ground as bullets from too-close-for-comfort Chinese troops who had broken through were fired from close range. The New Jerseyan fell on the dirty snow and grabbed the explosive in his hand, tossing it toward the nearby enemy. The explosion came quickly, ripping the private's finger off and sending shrapnel through his right hand and arm. The wounded marines near him lay in awe of the injured man who had just saved their lives, and Cafferata, now taking

Private Hector Cafferata Jr. waged a lone battle with grenades and rifle fire, holding a position against the invading Chinese in the northern mountains of North Korea. *Congressional Medal of Honor Society.*

his place next to them, himself all cut up, seemed to fit right in with the group. Yet, ignoring the pain, the young private picked up his rifle and stood back up, continuing to shield his fallen brothers in arms. American reinforcements continued pouring in each hour, finally clogging up the break in the line, previously held by a lone marine from New Jersey. Cafferata would have stayed to the end had a sniper's bullet not struck him and taken him out of the fight.

The New Jersey man never really talked about what happened on that hill, where the cold and the Chinese army almost got the best of him. Evacuated first to Japan in December and then stateside for treatment at the U.S. Naval Hospital at St. Albans, New York, Cafferata was officially declared "retired" on September 1, 1951. The war was still waging in Korea when President Truman presented the man with his Medal of Honor on November 24, 1952, almost two years after he found himself holding a strip of land against thousands of oncoming enemy soldiers. Hector never talked much about his time near the Chosin Reservoir, where he became one of the "Chosin Few," as the survivors would be labeled.

Hector politely turned down many requests for interviews from local papers and civic organizations for the remainder of his life, only speaking sporadically about his wartime experience.[227] His children would not know of the Congressional Medal of Honor until sixteen years after he received it. Cafferata's mother once recalled, "He didn't talk about it after the war… it was too horrible.…He did talk a bit later, and from some of the things he told me, I can understand why he didn't talk."[228] Ironically, his citation credited the young man with only fifteen kills. His commanding officer feared that if he logged the actual number of more than one hundred, Cafferata might be turned down for the commendation because nobody would believe it.[229]

Hector, who had also earned the Purple Heart and the Bronze Star, eventually relocated to Florida. He would sometimes visit the Hector A. Cafferata Elementary School in Fort Myers, named in his honor, to talk to young children about the importance of service. He passed away surrounded by his family on April 12, 2016.

"It was waves of fear and fighting panic," former private Hector A. Cafferata would say late into his adult life when recalling the events of that November night. "You didn't have time to think. I don't think I gave any of it conscious thought. You have friends there who are wounded and hurt. You decide you have to stick it out. The thought of leaving never occurred to me. Besides, you couldn't run very far without running into more Chinese." He then added, "Your fear is telling you, 'Let's get the hell out of here.' Your brain is telling you, 'There's no place to hide, you've got a choice—kill or be killed.'"[230]

The Battle for Chosin was a turning point for the American military situation in Korea. The white-clad Chinese kept coming no matter how much the marines and the army tried holding on to their line. Day after day, from the night of November 27 to December 13, the Americans heard the blaring bugles and watched thousands of Chinese descend on their positions. When a Chinese soldier went down, veterans would later recall, dozens more suddenly appeared.[231] By early December, the American and United Nations forces were fighting in the opposite direction—battling for a way to get out. To this day, many historians regard the Battle of Chosin Reservoir as the most brutal in modern warfare history when accounting for violence, casualty rate, weather conditions and endurance.[232] When the battle ended fourteen days after it started, with the American forces finally escaping the Chosin trap, seventeen men were awarded the Congressional Medal of Honor, and seventy-eight others received Service Cross Medals. It was the second most only to the Battle of the Bulge.[233]

# A GRENADE RUN

F ollowing the Battle of Chosin Reservoir in late 1950, the United Nations forces continued suffering losses and retreating across North Korea, again past the 38th parallel, where the war started, and once more losing South Korea's capital, Seoul, to the reinforced enemy. The very public firing of General Douglas MacArthur was still a month away, as the United Nations set forth the plan for Operation Ripper, intended to recapture Seoul, destroy as much of the Chinese army as possible and bring the troops back to the 38th parallel. For Sergeant Nelson V. Brittin, March 6, 1951, was just another start of a military operation, another D-Day of sorts, one he had seen plenty of before, in this war and the one before it. The difference, which he could not know, lay in the fact that he would not be coming home from this one.

Nelson was not new to war. After graduating from Audubon High School in New Jersey in 1938, the young man was drafted into the army within months of the United States' entrance into the Second World War. Having spent most of his time in Europe fighting in the Italian campaign—where he received two Purple Hearts—Brittin remained in Italy to study at a local college. Unable to find himself in the postwar world, the twenty-eight-year-old man reenlisted in the army in 1948 and was sent to Japan with the occupation forces. As luck would have it, Brittin's tour of duty saw him sent to South Korea on the eve of the war as part of a humanitarian effort, where he taught local children English.[234] His world changed once again on June 25, 1950. After years of tension between the democratic South and

The Korean War Memorial along the boardwalk in Atlantic City, New Jersey. *Library of Congress.*

the Communist North, the North Korean People's Army crossed the 38th parallel separating the divided peninsula and invaded South Korea.

Fighting with the 3rd Battalion, 19th Infantry Regiment, and 24th Infantry Division, Brittin found himself among the first American responders to the North Korean aggression. Because the division was the closest to the unfolding events, with some units in South Korea and others in nearby Japan, it became the first one to respond. Its mission, to take the initial brunt of the attack and try and slow down the enemy's progress long enough for United Nations reinforcements to arrive, had cost the division ten thousand casualties in the first few months of the conflict. Wounded in battle in December 1950 and then in February 1951, Sergeant First Class Nelson Brittin added two additional Purple Hearts to the ones he received during World War II. And while the recent months witnessed the Americans "advancing in another direction," as famously stated by General Oliver P. Smith, it was now time to go on the offensive.

On April 7, 1951, Brittin's battalion was tasked with advancing to a segment of the enemy front eight miles east of Seoul, codenamed the "Idaho Line." The weather was erratic, with great banks of clouds coming over since the previous day, limiting any ability to make good use of American air superiority.[235] The sergeant from New Jersey's Camden County volunteered to lead his squad up a nearby hill after the largest American artillery bombardment of the entire war opened the fighting. The Chinese and North Korean armies returned fire immediately, albeit a bit quieter and with less verve than Company I, 3rd Battalion, expected. The enemy wanted the initial attack to go well. The more the Americans succeeded in the first stage of the drive, the more isolated their units would be when the Chinese counterattacked.[236]

After they started up a hill circled on their military maps, and in relative safety for the first portion of their journey, the hidden enemy gun emplacements sprang up seemingly out of nowhere. The men scattered in search of cover that refused to materialize apart from some large rocks and sporadic charred trees. Curling up into fetal positions and tucking their heads to their chests, the men waited for a break that was not coming. When enemy artillery began supplementing the machine gun fire, it was more than evident to Sergeant Brittin that staying in the exposed position meant certain death. The sergeant volunteered to move his squad farther up the hill and neutralize the nearest gun emplacement. The idea proved to be more complex than previously imagined, as the extensive and relentless machine gun fire hindered any significant movement. Temporarily shielded by a large rock, Brittin signaled for his men to cover him. Hanging his M1 rifle by its strap across his chest, the New Jersey man unpinned a hand grenade and moved out of cover.

His men followed their orders with precision and vigor, shooting at everything around the young man now running in a zigzag pattern toward the enemy. When finally near, Brittin hurled his grenade and fell to the ground, covering his helmet with his hands. After picking his head up and realizing the success of his daring charge, the World War II vet set back for his initial position. Just as he was about to reach it, an explosion from an enemy grenade threw his body into the air, crashing to the ground as a child might do with their G.I. Joe figurine. Undeterred, the injured sergeant stood right up and continued his retreat. Within the few minutes it took for a medic to get to Brittin, the thirty-year-old man was already setting back toward the enemy positions. A satchel full of the grenades his men were willing to share with him hung across his chest, and a long bayonet was attached to the point of his rifle.

The squad continued moving up the enemy-held hillside, this time with the New Jersey man ahead of them. With the U.S. soldiers covering his every move, Brittin ran from enemy position to enemy position, tossing grenades and picking off any Chinese survivors attempting to move entrenchments with his Garand rifle. The sergeant still had the M1 in his hand when he came upon another shallow foxhole with two enemy soldiers. Brittin quickly raised his rifle to fire, but to his dismay, the gun jammed. The enemy soldiers paused when they saw the American with his rifle pointed at them, and before they could realize what had just transpired, Nelson was already in the foxhole using his bayonet and the butt of the M1 to kill them. There was no other option. When it is war, one does not brag about a kill or get excited about it. Killing the enemy is different; if one hesitates, the enemy will kill them—or worse, kill the soldier standing next to them.

Sergeant First Class Nelson Brittin charged enemy positions with a bag full of grenades during the war in Korea. *Congressional Medal of Honor Society.*

Brittin stepped out of the foxhole and looked back, realizing that a nearby enemy emplacement had pinned down his squad and that he was ahead of everyone else, alone, surrounded by the Chinese. The New Jerseyan moved down the hill two steps at a time toward the back of the machine gun position he passed before while racing up the hill. When he was right upon them, he tossed in a grenade. He had done this quite a lot that afternoon and already knew what to expect. Instead of stopping, Brittin continued his run ahead to the front of the emplacement and, using his rifle, picked out the three enemy soldiers trying to escape the explosion. The clip, signaling that he was out of ammo, pinged loudly as it flew off the rifle. Brittin reloaded the weapon and waited for his squad to catch up.

While together again, the men advanced for nearly one hundred yards to the mountain's summit before coming upon a much more organized, camouflaged and sandbagged machine gun nest. As the enemy fire rained on the advancing Americans, a group of well-hidden Chinese riflemen on each side and slightly above the hill covered every inch of the ground Brittin's men hoped to attain. Once more, the men looked to their sergeant to help them forward, and he obliged. Brittin reached into his bag of grenades and rushed forward. The burst of heavy machine gunfire cut him down before he ever made it anywhere near the emplacement. His men did not even have the chance to start firing their weapons to cover his advance—it was over before it started. The hill that claimed Sergeant Brittin's life—a mark on someone's map, part of a made-up line drawn out in marker and ordered to be taken, a small piece of the larger fight to reclaim Seoul—is now all but forgotten. It has become insignificant, except to those who gave their lives trying to seize it and, perhaps, those who lived to tell about it because of the sacrifices of men like Nelson V. Brittin. The New Jerseyan's body was returned to his hometown in November 1951 and buried at Beverly National Cemetery in Beverly, New Jersey. A Veterans of Foreign Wars (VFW) post in his hometown now bears his name.

Secretary of Defense Robert Lovett presented Brittin's Medal of Honor to his mother in a ceremony inside the Pentagon on January 16, 1952.[237] By then, Seoul was back in American and United Nations hands, General MacArthur was no longer leading the charge and the American troops settled into a stalemate on the 38th parallel—the location of the initial North Korean invasion that started the conflict two years before. As of 2023, there are still thirty thousand American military personnel in Korea, what some foreign pundits call "America's Forever War."[238] For the people back home in the United States, the conflict has taken on another moniker: the "Forgotten War." A sad legacy for Sergeant Brittin and the other 36,673 Americans who lost their lives in the line of duty fighting for their country in Korea.

More than 1 million Americans served in Korea, where the nation's first so-called unwinnable war was fought.[239] Historians, and sometimes veterans, would write much about the conflict, what would have happened if we never got involved or never moved up the peninsula toward the Incheon River and the Chinese border, or if General MacArthur had his way and dropped atomic bombs on targets in China and North Korea. The soldiers who came home after July 27, 1953—Armistice Day between North and South Korea, which returned the peninsula to its divided status quo—were not given many parades. Instead, they seemed to want to forget the whole thing, and the rest of the decade was busy enough to help them do just that.[240] Newspapers and television concentrated on the decade's economic prosperity, the "I Like Ike" enthusiasm, the civil rights movement, juvenile delinquency and the Space Race. But for those who read past the front page, the clues of another conflict were plain to see. When President Dwight Eisenhower sent the first military advisers to Indochina in 1955, the average American had never heard of Vietnam— within another decade, they would never be able to forget it.

# GUARDIAN ANGELS

**V**ietnam, Vietnam....There are no sure answers," wrote the veteran Southeast Asian correspondent Robert Shaplen about what he called "a perplexing period of a long and confusing war."[241] Yet, as Philip Caputo said in his memoir of the Vietnam War, the conflict changes when seen through the eyes of the soldiers who fought it. The stories about war, what men do in war and the things that war does to them "have nothing to do with politics, power, strategy, influence, national interests, or foreign policy."[242] They are also "not an indictment of the great men who led [men] into Indochina and whose mistakes were paid with the blood of some quite ordinary men." Stories of men such as Jedh Barker, Peter Connor or Charles Hosking speak about sacrifice, duty and the pride of being born in a nation and to the generation that defeated evil in World War II. They present the youthful ideas of nobility, goodness and the understanding that service above one's self is the creed of the American republic.

As Theodore Roosevelt once famously stated, "It is not the critic who counts; not the man who points out how the strong man stumbles, or where the doer of deeds could have done them better. The credit belongs to the man who is actually in the arena, whose face is marred by dust and sweat and blood; who strives valiantly, who errs, who comes short again and again, because there is no effort without error and shortcoming; but who does actually strive to do the deeds; who knows great enthusiasms, the great devotions, who spends himself in a worthy cause; who at best knows, in the end, the triumph of high achievement, and who at worst, if he fails, at least fails while daring greatly, so that his place shall never be with those cold and timid souls who neither know victory nor defeat."[243]

Nearly 250 people packed the Park Ridge High School Auditorium on November 31, 1969—a place Jedh C. Barker once called his second home. For four years, the crowds cheered every time the basketball star sank a basket. It was much the same with baseball, football and track, where Jedh captained his school to victories. But on that cold fall day, they all gathered in silence. The people listened to a local VFW commander's caution about forgetting wars, specifically the sacrifices of the young men fighting. They watched in silence as the mayor presented Mr. and Mrs. Barker with a plaque commemorating their deceased son, the first Bergen County resident to receive the Congressional Medal of Honor in Vietnam.[244] It had been nearly two years since the twenty-two-year-old Jedh gave his life fighting in Southeast Asia. His war was not conventional, with dramatic campaigns and historical battles, but one fought in the jungle, with monotonous ambushes and firefights—still, it was the only one he knew.[245] As another plaque was mounted on the school wall, another veteran from a different war, in another time when people back home celebrated duty and sacrifice, led the crowd in singing the national anthem. And then they all went home.

CPl. JEDH BARKER
Honor -- In Death

**Parents Accept Highest Award For Heroic Son**

Jedh Barker's ultimate sacrifice in Vietnam saw to it that it was his parents who had to accept his medal for valor. *From the* Paterson Morning Call, *1969.*

Lance Corporal Jedh C. Barker of Park Ridge, New Jersey, arrived in Vietnam with his brother, Lieutenant Colonel Warren C. Barker, in early 1967. At the time, the American intervention in the region was aimed at containing North Vietnamese Communism and ridding the South of Communist forces, the Viet Cong. By the time the brothers arrived, the conflict had dragged on without the quick victory promised to the American people back home. With the controversial draft and growing casualty numbers, the war was tearing the United States' social fabric. None of this stopped Jedh and Warren. The Barker brothers served in the same battalion within the 2nd Marine Regiment, 3rd Division, an important distinction, as it was also the same battalion their father served in during the Second World War. The twenty-two-year-old Jedh understood the importance of honor and duty to one's nation, a legacy passed onto him through his father. The lance corporal's unusual first name was made up of four of his father's World War II buddies—John, Ezekiel, Donald and Herbert—once all members of the same unit he now proudly served.[246]

It must have become evident to the young New Jerseyan from the moment he landed in Vietnam that this would not be his father's war. There would be no epic clashes whose outcomes would decide the fates of armies and nations. "The war was mostly a matter of enduring weeks of expectant waiting and, at random intervals, of conducting vicious manhunts through jungles and swamps where snipers harassed us constantly and booby traps cut us down one by one," Caputo wrote. "The tedium was occasionally relieved by large search-and-destroy operations…but those were usually more or the same hot walking, with the mud sucking at our boots and the sun thudding against our helmets while the invisible enemy shot at us from distant tree lines."[247]

The U.S. Marine Corps military base in Con Thien was located near the Demilitarized Zone (DMZ), separating Democratic South Vietnam from the Communist North. It was also less than two miles from North Vietnam's Quang Tri Province. Jedh's 3rd Marine Division's job was to keep the Con Thien secure to prevent any North Vietnamese Army penetration of the DMZ. A cluster of three small hills, some as high as 150 meters, formed the American position. While it provided perfect views for ten miles into North Vietnam, it also opened the marines to enemy artillery. Former lance corporal Jack T. Hartzel with Jedh Barker's 3rd Division did not mince any words when he called Con Thien "an ugly, bare patch of red mud."[248] The locals had their own name for it, the "Hill of the Angels," due to the massive number of casualties it absorbed.

Because of the hill's size, only one reinforced battalion could hold the position. To remedy the issue, two other peaks, the Dong Ha to the south and the Gio Linh to the northeast, supported the overall mission to stop any advances. Had the North Vietnamese Army (NVA) overrun any of the three defensive positions, it would have a clear road to the south. "We would run patrols and ambushes every day to keep the NVA on the move. We wanted to make certain they couldn't build fixed positions in and around the area." Hartzel remembered it not being an easy job. "We would destroy a bunker complex one day, and a couple of days later, it would be rebuilt—some as close as 1,500 meters to Con Thien."[249] The bigger problem for men like Hartzel or Barker was not the fact that the area to patrol was too large and that the NVA could move freely without much detection—it was the constant shelling.

Had he returned home to tell his story, the New Jersey man would have undoubtedly agreed with his friends' assessment of calling Con Thien "Our Turn in the Barrel" or "The Meatgrinder." The shelling worsened in September 1967, with daily drops of more than two hundred artillery rounds. From September 19 to September 27, more than three thousand rounds hit the Con Thien Marine Base. "I will never forget [those days]," a marine recalled. "We took over 1,200 rounds that day with hardly a spot on the hill not hit by an incoming round of some sort."[250] Because the area hit was so small, there was virtually no place for the marines to hide. If that were not enough, the NVA would probe the hills each night to find any weaknesses in the American lines. The continued shelling, night attacks and daily patrol missions were taking their toll on the soldiers' mental and physical health—this was Vietnam.

Apart from the extra shelling that started two days before, September 21, 1967, was just like any other day in Con Thien, when Lance Corporal Jedh C. Barker, serving as a machine gunner, set off on a reconnaissance operation with Company F in and around the marine military base. Deploying to combat formation, the men advanced through the thick jungle at the mercy of the mosquitos and the inevitable NVA units roaming the area. As was usually the case, the company did not have to move too far off base to come across the enemy position. "We would patrol an area," Hartzel wrote, "and they would return as soon as we were gone."[251] Jedh dropped to the ground as small-arms and machine gun fire ripped through the trees around him. It was often the same—fierce fighting without much visibility, people dying without much opportunity to return the favor. The adrenaline made the soldiers seem invincible for those five minutes, or at least unaware of their own fragility. Corporal Barker's M60 machine gun, often called the "pig," faithfully fulfilled its purpose as it spat out 7.62mm rounds, sounding very much like the uncontrollable grunts of a barnyard hog. According to the letter later sent to his father by a fellow marine, Jedh did not even realize he had been hit.[252]

Pinned by Barker's fire, the NVA shifted its attack toward the New Jersey man's position. Jedh remained in the open, picking out those enemy soldiers he could and firing blindly in their general direction when he could not see a thing. The second round that hit him ripped through his hand. A fellow marine grabbed the protesting lance corporal and dragged him away from the fight. Now twice wounded, Barker refused an evacuation, even though the loss of blood was catching up to him, weakening him by the minute. Jedh half lay and half sat next to another badly hurt marine as a corpsman was finishing up sticking him with morphine. None of the men noticed the sole NVA man sneak up to their position, and likely none of them but Jedh saw the grenade land right by their feet.

Grenade training often begins with basics, assuming the to-be soldier does not know how to throw a baseball correctly. Yet if an activated grenade does find its way near a person, the best advice would be to run or get as far away from the upcoming explosion. Some involve picking it up and throwing it away, kicking it as far as possible or, most commonly, if all else fails, covering it with a bag or a helmet to weaken its blast. What the basic training fails to stress is that grenades do not roll in slowly toward one's position; they are thrown with force, often bouncing around the ground—catching them or kicking them is impossible. Jedh and the men who had seen the horrors of war also likely knew that the five-second fuse was more like three seconds.

Many veterans, regardless of the conflict they fought in, have mentioned the friendship that develops between men who face danger and misery head on, day after day, with nobody but themselves to turn to—it is not something they teach you in training. It could be argued that Jedh Barker, at twenty-two years old, knew more about family, heartache and sacrifice than many of his contemporaries back home—loss, grief and desolation were his teachers. The New Jersey man got up and threw himself on the live grenade, his body absorbing the full and tremendous force of the explosion. "He died a hero so that two others could live," expressed the letter his father received weeks later. "Sir, for this, every man in the platoon and the C.O. wrote him up for the Medal of Honor. Our platoon commander says he'll get it. I certainly hope so." The letter was signed, "Bark's friend, Kerry."[253]

"The thing about [Con Thien] that really sticks in my mind," Lance Corporal Jack T. Hartzel wrote, "is a picture of a Marine sitting in a puddle of blood and battle dressings, on a poncho, with his legs blown off from the waist down! He was numb from morphine and in shock from loss of blood." The former marine added, "He was smoking a cigarette very calmly as if nothing had even happened! He was waiting for a Medevac. He probably died in the chopper ride back." In his final assessment of September 1967 and the days when Jedh Barker lost his life, the marine wrote, "Our platoon arrived at Con Thien with forty-five men; when we left, we only had twelve. Now you know why we called it 'The Meatgrinder.'"[254]

It was a warm Tuesday, May 2, 1967, in the White House Rose Garden. The six-foot-four Lyndon B. Johnson walked up to the petite Eleanor M. Connor, who wore a simple white dress, and her even smaller eight-year-old daughter, Cecilia, dressed in yellow and black. The commander-in-chief hung the gold and bronze Medal of Honor around the mother's neck and turned to the assembled crowd. "Sergeant Connor," the president began, "died at a time of testing, not only for himself but for his country. Thousands of miles away from the battlefield on which he fell, his countrymen debate the course of the war he fought in." Johnson paused and looked up before glancing back down at his notes. "The debate will go on, so long as men like Peter Connor shoulder their packs and face—not hostile placards and debating points—but the bullets and mortar shells of aggressive armies," said the president. "The debate will go on, and it will have its price. It is a price our democracy must be prepared to pay and that the angriest voices of dissent should be prepared to acknowledge."[255]

It was a poignant political speech, but to Mrs. Connor, no political or unifying message would bring back her husband. It might have been the price the nation's democracy was prepared to pay, but was she?

In February 1966, the thirty-three-year-old Peter Spencer Connor, born and raised in South Orange, New Jersey, was far from anything resembling home. When he arrived in Vietnam with the 2nd Battalion, 3rd Marines, 1st Marine Division, it was apparent that none of the guys there was looking for

President Johnson presents the Medal of Honor to widow and daughter of Marine Corps sergeant Peter S. Connor. *From the* Paterson Morning Call, *1969.*

new friends; too many of theirs had already died. The Viet Cong (VC), a pro–
North Vietnam guerrilla force operating throughout the South, had quickly
learned that fighting the American full military strength in the open deltas, rice
patties and stretches of the jungle was too costly. The new VC strategy called
for surprise ambushes with hit-and-run tactics. For an average soldier such
as Staff Sergeant Peter Connor, it turned the war into short, sometimes only
ten-minute battles, where if one survived the first fifteen seconds, they would
likely live another day. Peter's new daily reality revolved around a new military
strategy of "search and destroy," where helicopters would drop smaller units
of Americans into various areas and send them to find the enemy.

Douglass Anderson, also of the 3rd Marines, 1st Marine Division, later
wrote, "The very idea of the search and destroy operation is one of enormous
logical fallacy. You send a patrol out in order to get it ambushed in order to
mark a target with a smoke rocket from a helicopter so jets can come in and
napalm the area. In other words, you have to get ambushed before you can
find the enemy." The VC was smart enough to know that it would take three
to five minutes for the air support to get there, "so they could kill a couple of
people and split before anybody ever got there."[256] Who is to say if Sergeant
Connor would ever want to talk about the daily life in Vietnam once he got
home to his wife and daughter? The heat, the insects, the snakes and the
people trying to kill you daily must have left an impression on him as much
as it did on those who came home to tell the tale or, as was often the case,
never mention it again.

The only thing providing the American soldier some comfort was the
knowledge that the men next to him would look out for him as much as
he would for them. For Peter, as well as for others, any search-and-destroy
mission had with it a certain level of danger or unpredictability. "The Viet
Cong would be a farmer you waved to from your jeep in the day who would
be the guy with the gun out looking for you at night," recalled a medic with
the 1st Infantry. "They would come together and man a small offensive or
probe attack, drop a few mortar rounds, and go home and call it a night."[257]
The biggest frustration was trying to determine who was Viet Cong and
who was not. Moreover, because the VC had created a hidden system of
tunnels that stretched for hundreds of miles, it was nearly impossible to find
the enemy hiding in crevices, tunnels and holes in the ground—there one
second and gone another.

In typical Viet Cong fashion, the small-arms fire came at Staff Sergeant
Connor's platoon as it often did, fast and already fleeting. As the men fanned
out, it became evident that the marines had come upon an area full of

Peter S. Connor lost his life protecting his fellow marines from a faulty grenade. *Congressional Medal of Honor Society.*

traps and a few tunnel entrances. The former was particularly bad. "We took more casualties from booby traps than we did from actual combat," remembered a veteran. "It was very frustrating because how do you fight back against a booby trap? You're just walking along, and all of a sudden, your buddy doesn't have a leg."[258] As Connor maneuvered his unit aggressively toward the Viet Cong fire, he noticed an enemy spider hole about forty feet ahead. Before a VC could come back up from the hidden position in the ground and bring about more death, the staff sergeant let his M16 rifle dangle from its sling and pulled the pin out of one of his grenades. Peter took one step toward the enemy emplacement when he realized that although he held the explosive's safety device firmly in its place, the grenade was faulty in that its fuse charge was already activated.

Looking around, the husband and father from New Jersey likely saw his platoon mates firing ferociously at the enemy right near him. There was no time to make it to the VC spider hole, and throwing the grenade in any direction would surely mean killing a fellow marine. Peter tucked the grenade close to his body and closed his eyes. He would never open them again—taking his last breath on March 8, 1966, on board the hospital ship the USS *Repose*. As the ship's designation suggested, he would now rest forever in peace and tranquility. The war, however, went on.

SOME INDIVIDUALS ARE MEANT to wear a uniform—they do not take "no" for an answer or accept a life without service. Master Sergeant Charles E. Hosking Jr. of the U.S. Army was such a man. Shortly after the breakout of World War II in Europe in September 1939, and before the United States' entrance, Charles failed to show up for his classes at Ramsey High School. To the dismay of his parents, the young Hosking had run away from home. The goal was to join the Canadian army in Montreal and fight against Germany, and he almost succeeded before the authorities discovered that he was only sixteen. A disappointed Hosking returned to New Jersey and his high school only to leave again, this time with his parents' knowledge, in 1942 to join the U.S. Coast Guard. He was seventeen and finally able to pursue what he believed to be his calling: serving his country.

By the time Hosking returned to Vietnam for his third tour of duty many years after World War II had ended, his reputation had already preceded him. The large-statured, forty-two-year-old master sergeant with five combat campaign stars, the Bronze Star, the Purple Heart and three Presidential Unit Citations was a minor celebrity among his Special Forces group.[259] His men knew him as "Snake" because he could slide in and out of difficult situations virtually unscathed. The World War II veteran, who back in the 1940s served with the 82nd Airborne Division, fought in some of the worst battles of the infamous conflict. When his 1,500-men battalion disbanded after partaking in the Battle of the Bulge, the badly wounded Hosking was one of only 30 surviving members.[260] Although active through the Korean War, a bazooka training accident prevented Charles from seeing combat and kept him stateside.

Charles Hosking was first sent to Vietnam as a military adviser to local Special Forces in 1961. Picked for his demolition expertise and ability to speak numerous languages, including German and Vietnamese, the Green Beret was the perfect choice to lead the new Civilian Irregular Defense Group Reaction Battalion. Designed by the Central Intelligence Agency (CIA) to counter the Viet Cong, these irregular Vietnamese military units, comprising local villagers and led by American military advisers, fought more clandestine battles against their Communist counterparts. In this capacity, the New Jersey father of four would end his service in the United States' most controversial conflicts.

Master Sergeant Hosking and his III Corps Defense Group Reaction Battalion arrived in the Don Luan District on March 21, 1967, two miles outside their Special Forces camp and west of Saigon, to investigate a growing Viet Cong presence in the area. At first, the bicycle-riding man was not out of place, but something seemed off enough for one of Hosking's men to stop and question the rider. After a roadside interrogation, the short man was identified as a VC sniper, which he arrogantly admitted. Charles ordered his men to arrest the enemy soldier and bring him in for further questioning at their camp. As the other battalion members moved toward the M151 MUTT light utility vehicle, the New Jersey

Charles Hosking Jr. did not hesitate when he tackled an enemy soldier wielding a live grenade. *Congressional Medal of Honor Society.*

man untied the Viet Cong's hands, previously tied together by a Vietnamese member of the Defense Group. One could only speculate, and many have, why Charles would do that—perhaps it was the knowledge that the man was searched and possessed no weapons to hurt anyone, but that is a mere guess.

The VC man seized the moment and, in a split second, ripped a grenade from Hosking's belt. Instead of staying close to the large and intimidating New Jersey man, the enemy lurched toward Charles's company command group—two American and two Vietnamese soldiers who stood just to the side and near the jeep. Perhaps the scenario of what was about to transpire played out in his head, or there was no time to think but only to react. Regardless of what the forty-two-year-old Hosking felt at that moment, the sergeant completely disregarded his safety and leaped on the Viet Cong's back. As the two hit the ground, the larger man pinned the enemy in a bear hug, forcing the grenade against the VC's chest. The men near them turned around, and before they could do anything to stop it, the explosive blasted their sergeant and the enemy. By the time they got down to Charles, it was too late; he had sacrificed his life so they could go on with theirs.

Another little boy standing in the Oval Office might have been too young to understand the seriousness of the situation, but not the eight-year-old Wesley Hosking. Dressed in a suit and a little bowtie, the young boy stepped toward the president of the United States as his mother, Gloria, and three sisters stood silently watching. Their ceremony was not open to the public in the Rose Garden; it was a private affair inside the White House. Richard Nixon bent down and handed Wesley a wooden box with a glass front; inside was his father's Congressional Medal of Honor. The boy thanked the president and looked up at the nearby camera. *Click*—not much to smile about, especially for a little boy who lost his father.

Within two months, President Nixon announced the withdrawal of sixty thousand American troops from Vietnam as part of his "Vietnamization" and "Peace with Honor" initiatives of starting to hand control of the fight over to the local South Vietnamese Army. By the afternoon of May 23, 1969, when Wesely accepted his father's medal, more than forty thousand American soldiers had already lost their lives in the jungles of Vietnam. This medal and the other twenty-two handed out by Richard Nixon were as much for the men whose citations accompanied the decoration as a testament for those who never came home, came back broken or had yet to see the horrors of Vietnam. U.S. combat troops would not leave Southeast Asia for another four years, until March 19, 1973.

# IF NOT YOU, THEN WHO?

The world around him went in and out of focus. The first lieutenant might have walked, crawled or floated. He opened his eyes; large rotating helicopter blades interrupted the tranquil blue sky above him. Jack was on his back—being carried and placed inside the machine's metal hull. The bullets whizzed past him, bouncing off the Bell UH-1 (Huey) helicopter. He could hear the engine struggling under the relentless enemy machine gun fire. Then it lifted off the ground. The twenty-two-year-old Jack H. Jacobs of Woodbridge, New Jersey, just survived an hour that, against his intent, would make him known forever.

"In the heat of the battle, soldiers do not think of valor, do not rate acts of brotherhood or compassion or soldierly virtue," Colonel Jack Howard Jacobs later wrote. "It is the moral courage that drives the great events of our lives…the act of doing the right thing when it is much easier to do otherwise."[261] The man, whom a superior officer would later call "a little tiger" and credit him with saving an entire battalion, grew up in a middle-class, hardworking Jewish family from New Jersey.[262] Jacobs's parents, his father a former U.S. Army Signal Corps soldier during the Second World War, taught Jack from a very young age to "develop a seriousness of purpose and a strong sense of responsibility." And although the small-statured youth took his time fully embracing the message while growing up, especially through his early years in school, his parents never had to tell Jack to work hard.[263] In the jungles of Vietnam on March 9, 1968, there was little doubt that the message had fully sunk in.

The then first lieutenant Jack H. Jacobs ignored life-threatening wounds to his head to help save his unit during intense fighting in Vietnam. *Congressional Medal of Honor Society.*

Jacobs graduated from the Reserve Officers' Training Corps (ROTC) program at Rutgers University in 1966, just months shy of his twenty-first birthday. The Vietnam War headed toward its peak of U.S. involvement, with 300,000 troops and sailors stationed in Southeast Asia and American deaths from the conflict totaling 6,000. Back home, the antiwar movement was gaining momentum and national media attention—the 100,000-strong antiwar protest on the steps of the Lincoln Memorial was just one year away. The young officer from New Jersey saw things differently. "The freedom that we enjoy today," Jacobs later wrote, "has been purchased with the blood and sacrifice of countless men and women who were simply doing the right thing, what they were supposed to do, when they needed to do it." In the summer of 1966, doing the right thing for an officer of the U.S. Army meant fighting alongside his men, in Jack's case the 82nd Airborne Division.

In a twist of fate, the Infantry Branch instead selected him to go to Vietnam as a military adviser to a Vietnamese unit. In the end, it was his college degree that made him "uniquely qualified" for the assignment.[264] The young New Jerseyan arrived at an airfield in Vietnam in 1967, greeted by troops who had just finished their tour of duty and were awaiting their transport back home. "We got off, and going on the plane were soldiers who looked like they were one hundred years old." Jack looked on in amazement at what a few months in the jungle had done to these nineteen- or twenty-year-olds—he would look just like them within eight weeks. James Bombard, a rifle platoon leader of the 101st Airborne Division, would later speak about this phenomenon of "boys with men's faces." Often all it took to get the green kids up to speed was their first firefight. "Usually, the first firefight consisted not only of a fight but also so many days in the jungle putting the skills of a soldier to use—walking in the jungle, being scared, setting up defenses, perimeters. It was thinking about survival, and all of the sudden, BOOM, you were a soldier, you were a veteran."[265]

The young New Jersey officer arrived in Vietnam right in time for one of the most controversial periods of the entire conflict: the Tet Offensive.

After years of defensive war, the Viet Cong decided to use the Lunar New Year holiday period to launch a wide-scale offensive on major urban and American-controlled centers in South Vietnam. The Communists' large and coordinated last-ditch effort on January 30, 1968, was akin to Hitler's Battle of the Bulge and was meant to disorient the American and South Vietnamese forces. In a best-case scenario, it would topple the South's government while inflicting enough casualties to sour the American public's opinion of the conflict and pressure the government to withdraw its military. The Tet Offensive continued for nearly a month before U.S. forces regained control and began pursuing the responsible VC enemy units. And although General William Westmoreland's declaration that the offensive was a terrible defeat for the enemy was correct, his claim could not be any further from the truth when considering its effect on the American psyche and political structure back home.

It did not matter that the Viet Cong lost thirty-two thousand men in the offensive and the Americans slightly more than three thousand.[266] The tide at home turned for the worst when Walter Cronkite, one of the nation's most respected journalists, broke character on television and rejected the administration's optimism toward the conflict. Looking into the camera, Cronkite, who had visited Vietnam during the Tet Offensive, told the American people that the war was unwinnable, stating that it was "more certain than ever that the bloody experience of Vietnam is to end in a

The U.S. military adopted the "search and destroy" strategy to counter the unconventional nature of the conflict. *Public Broadcasting Service.*

stalemate."[267] While President Johnson's popularity plummeted, the polls soon reflected the almost even break between the hawks and doves. The year 1968 would prove pivotal to the entire conflict and change the nation's course. But for those on the ground, none of that mattered. They had a job to do, and politics was not even remotely in its description.

A few weeks after Cronkite's address and the regaining of American control over the hard-hit areas from the Tet Offensive, First Lieutenant Jacobs and his South Vietnamese unit continued their pursuit of the enemy. The Kien Phong Province Headquarters had recently received some intelligence information about the location of the headquarters of the enemy unit Jack and his men had been chasing and fighting since the Tet. The March 9, 1968 operation called for a two-pronged attack. The New Jersey man's South Vietnamese 2nd Battalion, 16th Infantry Regiment, 9th Infantry Division, moved into position from assault boats on the north bank of the Bassac River. At the same time, helicopters dropped an additional Vietnamese unit to approach the enemy from the opposite direction. None of the men knew at the time that a spy within the headquarters had shared the plan with the Viet Cong. Jack and his men were walking into an ambush.

The three hundred well-entrenched and armed enemy soldiers waited patiently. It was 8:30 a.m., and the sun was already unbearable, yet Jack and his men marched forward to their objective, tired and thirsty. The hope that scouts, presumably ahead of them, would provide ample warning of any contact with the Viet Cong provided some comfort. And then, just like that, the enemy machine gun fire and mortars sprang at them with relentless fury—quickly dissipating any such notions.

Close to seventy-five men dropped to the ground in mere seconds, some never to get up again, while others would carry the scars of battle with them until the rest of their days. Thousands of little jagged and sharp shards exploded among Jacobs and his men before they could register the whooshing sound of the incoming mortar shell. The force of the explosion instantly killed two of his men while ferociously throwing Jacobs and his noncommissioned (NCO) officer, Ray Ramirez, to the ground. Jack opened his eyes with difficulty, blood pouring out of his head wound, to see the NCO half standing and half sitting, struggling with a radio handset. Ramirez had injuries to his chest that were deflating his lungs, shrapnel in his abdomen and blood pouring out of his nose and mouth.[268]

Calling back the senior adviser with the battalion commander farther to the rear, Ramirez yelled into the handset, "This is 32 Charlie, 32 Alpha [referring to Jack] is hit real bad, and I do not think he is going to make it!"

Having finished his statement, the NCO fell back, unconscious. Jack rolled over to Ramirez and picked up the radio headset. "This is 32 Alpha, 32 Charlie is hit real bad, and I do not think he is going to make it!" The major on the other side of the radio barked back, "What is this a comedy routine? You guys get back to work!"[269] Jack grabbed his med kit and patched Ray up as best and as quickly as he could. While at it, he reached back toward his bloodsoaked head, now reminiscent of a moon's surface, and did the same.

The firefight still raged around him as the badly wounded Jack sought and found a nearby tree line among the open rice paddies and low dikes. Staying low to the ground while making his way toward potential refuge, he came across an injured young soldier, only to witness a mortar kill him an instant later. The situation around him was rapidly headed from bad to worse. Jacobs tried dragging one of his wounded battalion officers along with him toward safety, only to find out that the man was already safe—he would never have to worry about anything ever again on this earth. The constant thunder of artillery and bullets reminded Jack that time was of the essence—they were pinned down and in danger of being overrun by the Viet Cong, a sure death sentence. With the company commander down, the men began to panic. Jacobs grabbed the radio and called in airstrikes on the enemy positions, all while realizing that they were too close for comfort.[270] Jack saw only one way out when the air support failed in their approach, chased away by enemy fire. The lieutenant took command, yelling for his men to withdraw toward the tree line and establish a defensive perimeter.

"Time slows down; in battle, three minutes seems like a lifetime," Jack later wrote.[271] But at that moment, something needed to be done. "In the midst of the death and screaming and chaos, I remembered a famous anecdote... of the first-century Jewish sage Hillel the Elder; 'If I am not for myself, who will be for me? And if I am only for myself, then what am I? And if not now, when?'" With blood streaming down his face and the back of his neck, the words in his head were clear. "Jacobs, if not you, then who?"[272]

Once away from the fighting and in relative, albeit temporary, safety, the New Jerseyan turned toward a South Vietnamese machine gunner and two riflemen and directed them to cover fire as he returned into the chaos to get Ray. Jacobs then returned to his men, but only for a few brief moments, leaving once more, this time to destroy a hidden bunker by dodging the incoming close-range fire and killing the enemy inside with his grenade. Bullets snapped around him as the young man ran back to his defensive position. Jacobs shifted direction mid-run, grabbed an injured man and then dragged him toward the new defensive perimeter. Jack "did this over and over" with the riflemen covering him, "inching forward, rifles splitting, hauling wounded friends back."[273]

"Fueled by fear and the adrenaline it produces," Jack later recalled, "I ran, shot, carried, bled. I didn't reload but instead snatched abandoned weapons from the battlefield." Once the American officer was back in his new defensive perimeter, the irritated Viet Cong, robbed of an easy victory by one man, inched closer to Jacobs only to meet their end, courtesy of the New Jersey man's rifle. Realizing that the structure of the enemy's position in a linear defense along a canal made it easier for him to attack from the side, Jack continuously worked his way around, outflanking the Viet Cong and shooting them from a more deadly and advantageous vantage point. In the meantime, he continued moving the wounded men farther and farther away from the oncoming enemy. "I understand you've got wounded Americans down there," said a navy gunship pilot through the radio. "Roger, we do," Jacobs answered. After a brief exchange that ended with the New Jerseyan popping a smoke grenade into an open fire-swept field to mark his and his men's location, the man on the radio asked, "Where are the bad guys in relation to the purple smoke?" With the loud firefight around him, Jack yelled back into the receiver, "In the smoke! They are right here!" There was a pause on the other side, then, "Oh, that's not very good."[274]

It lasted about thirty minutes, but to Jack H. Jacobs, it felt like hours. Eventually, his severe head wounds got the best of him. The crack of

President Nixon stands with four Medal of Honor recipients during their ceremony. Captain Jack H. Jacobs is the second from the right. *From the* Central New Jersey Home News, *1969.*

bullets and explosions around him kept him awake, until even those could no longer do so. Jack slipped in and out of consciousness. His muscles and body went through the motions as his mind tried to register the arrival of reinforcements. And then the helicopter blades and the bloody face of his still-alive friend Ray lying next to him on the Huey's cold metal floor. And then nothing.

Apart from Ray Ramirez, Jacobs's actions also saved a wounded company commander and twelve other allied soldiers. But the young man from New Jersey, now a captain, was not yet done with Vietnam. After recovering from his wounds and receiving the Congressional Medal of Honor, Jacobs had to use some heavy persuasion for the military to allow him to return to a combat role in Southeast Asia, which he managed to do. By the time he finished his last tour of duty in Vietnam, the New Jersey man had received two Silver Stars, three Bronze Star Medals and two Purple Hearts. Jack retired from the army in 1987 with the rank of colonel. He wrote in his 2008 memoir, "Soldiers act not for the accolade but for the lives of their comrades, and every action that is cited for its extraordinary heroism is merely a proxy for all those forever lost in the midst of the battlefield."[275]

# THE ANGEL OF HILL 875

The Marine Corps A-4 Skyhawk attack jet made its fourth run, one thousand feet above the densely forested Hill 875, east of the Vietnam and Cambodia border. Below, in their foxholes, were the men of the 173rd Airborne Brigade. Surrounded, tired and most severely wounded, the men had been fighting the battle of their lives against the heavily entrenched North Vietnamese Army, giving no quarter. Raymond Zaccone looked up from his foxhole. "All day, the jets went across the ridge, but this one was going along it."[276] And then they all saw it. The A-4 barreled in on a shallow ten-degree angle at hundreds of miles per hour as two bombs detached themselves from the aircraft and headed right toward them.[277] The first projectile struck the ground right in the center of the 173rd position—a dud. The second bomb gained speed as it headed straight for the casualty collection point, where an unlikely source, a forty-year-old Major Charles Watters, a Catholic priest, helped the medics care for the most severely wounded men. The battalion's chaplain from Jersey City, New Jersey, and forty men around him would not survive the worst friendly fire accident of the entire Vietnam War.

To those who knew him, Charles Watters was a wonderful, spiritual and caring man—yet none would call him your typical priest,[278] apart from leading many youth groups and nonprofit organizations at his various stops, from Virgin Mary's Church of Paramus to St. Mary's Church in his hometown of Jersey City and lastly to St. Michael's in Cranford. "He was a sincere, very unassuming man in his priestly life," recalled another member of Charles's last parish, yet there was also another non-priestly side to the man. Father Watters was a licensed pilot with more than five hundred flying hours who loved spending his free time parachuting out of airplanes. In 1962, the five-foot-nine priest asked the archdiocese to sign the required papers that would allow him to join the Air National Guard, which it reluctantly approved.[279] Within one year, he became its chaplain. Watters entered the U.S. Army in the same capacity at Fort Dix, New Jersey, in 1964. By July 1966, the daring yet gentle man had been assigned to the Republic of Vietnam as part of Company A, 173rd Support Battalion, 173rd Airborne Brigade.[280]

It was not out of place for Father Watters to accompany the brigade's line units into the field, during which he became very close with the men, who also came to rely on his calmness during battle. In November 1967, after having just extended his stay by six months, the chaplain was asked to accompany the three companies of the 2nd Battalion, 503rd Infantry, on their newest mission to secure a densely forested hill designated as Hill 875. The area was suspected of shielding parts of the infamous Ho Chi Minh Trail, which brought military supplies and troops from North Vietnam to the south via neighboring Cambodia and Laos. As recently as the first week of November, scouts reported seeing a large force of the North Vietnamese Army (NVA) on the hilltop, and it was the men's job to confirm it.

Watters moved up the hill's southern side on November 19, 1967, along with the 2nd Battalion, with Delta and Charlie slightly ahead of Company Alpha. As they moved forward, the artillery and air support dropped explosives to soften the enemy. For the men on the ground, the visibility was less than ten yards, as the vegetation was so dense that even if the enemy were right before them, the Americans likely would not see the Vietnamese in their well-camouflaged hiding spots.[281] The two forward companies came to a clearing, unseen from air reconnaissance photos. The NVA camp looked like it housed hundreds of enemy soldiers, if not more. There was an aid station, a communications depot and, worse, fires with their ashes still aglow.

Father Charles J. Watters disregarded his personal safety in order to help wounded soldiers during one of the bloodiest battles of the Vietnam War. *Congressional Medal of Honor Society.*

Visibly nervous, the men hesitated when ordered to continue up the hill. Chaplain Watters, seeing the situation, asked the commanding officer if it would be ok if he led a short mass and served communion. Although it was still early in the day, no later than 10:00 a.m., it seemed like there was no better time to provide some comfort. "He was the only chaplain I ever saw going so close to the action with us, and even though I was not Catholic, I went to the morning mass—I figured I could use all the help I could get," recalled Stephen Welch.[282] When the mass was complete, the men picked up their rifles and set forth on their march up toward the hillcrest. It all seemed too quiet, too calm. Welch picked up the headset and radioed back to ask for permission to recon by fire—where he and his men would line up and shoot into the jungle they thought was watching them—he was denied on both tries. And then it opened up, and men started dropping.

The well-concealed enemy picked off the men of the 2nd Battalion at will, while the Americans could not locate the bunkers and trenches that unleashed death on them. "Everywhere I looked, men were dying," Raymond Zaccone later said. "A medic ran up to me and asked if I was ok. I blinked, and he already lay dead next to me."[283] The men stopped briefly, stunned by the loud bugle sound coming from behind their position—a sign of a North Vietnamese charge. Without a proper place to land air support because of the dense forest, Company A asked for axes and other sharp objects to be dropped near their position so they could clear a landing zone (LZ). Yet soon, they were suffering so many casualties that they abandoned their efforts and regrouped with the remnants of the Charlie and Delta Companies farther up the hill.

As the battle raged on for hours and the men, surrounded and cut off from any help, fought desperately to save themselves, Chaplain Watters completely disregarded his safety and, while unarmed and exposed, moved from man to man, providing first aid. It was not lost on the men hanging on to their dear lives and shooting into the jungle and the invisible enemy that their priest moved between friendly and enemy bullets as he dragged wounded men back and away from the fight. At one point, Watters saw a young paratrooper frozen in fear, with bullets whizzing past his head, standing like a pole in the middle of chaos. The chaplain ran toward the man and picked him up on his shoulders, carrying him away to safety. "Father Watters did not have to be there, but he would not leave his men," Zaccone remembered. "At one point, I looked over at Father Watters, and he had a wounded soldier on his lap, and he was giving him his last rites, and it just so happened that the sun was shining through the trees right at him—he looked up and smiled at me."[284]

Able to establish a defensive perimeter, the men dug foxholes with anything they could, including bayonets and their helmets. Later in the day,

U.S. Army chaplain Major Charles J. Watters conducting a field mass in Vietnam. *Seaton Hall University Archives.*

the NVA fire slowed down to a trickle for a reason the men themselves could not fathom. The Americans were low on ammo, food and water, yet for now, they were relatively safe. Having been able to call in air strikes on the enemy positions had forced the Vietnamese to remain in the safety of their heavy log bunkers, providing some respite for Watters and his men. "Father Watters approached me in my foxhole," recalled Bat O'Leary, "and asked me if I could use one of his holy water or wine, which he had in these two small plastic containers. I thanked him and told him to bring it to the medics."[285] By late afternoon, the casualty collection point was well established, in no small part thanks to the efforts of Father Watters, who continued bringing in more wounded soldiers by the minute so the medics could work on them.

The quiet was now only broken by men crying and whimpering in pain and the occasional small-arms fire from the NVA still hiding in their defensive positions, although for how long the men of the 2nd Battalion could not know. Chaplain Watters looked outside the temporary perimeter to see wounded men become targets for NVA rifles. Unable to hold back, even when a few men tried restraining him, the New Jersey priest repeatedly rushed forward, with machine gun and rifle fire kicking the ground around him, and grabbed the wounded men to bring them inside the perimeter. When he was satisfied that all men still alive were safe, the chaplain finally agreed to remain behind the defensive line.

The dusk was settling as Father Watters moved from wounded man to wounded man, helping the medics. He applied bandages to open wounds, obtained and served any available food and water and gave spiritual and mental strength and comfort.[286] Only a few men saw him continue sneaking in and out of the perimeter to obtain more provisions from those that now had plenty to spare. Unlike many men around him, Watters refused to lose hope, even when there was none left to find on Hill 875. Any reinforcements were still a whole day away, battling their way up through the enemy's flank.

And even then, who was to say that any of the 2nd Battalion would be left alive to welcome them? The men waited for the inevitable NVA attack—many wounded, starving and low on ammo. And then they heard the jet overhead making its dry runs over their position. Something looked off about this one, its direction not quite in line with all others that dropped their loads that day.

The bomb from the American Marine Corps A-4 attack jet landed directly on the American field hospital position. Father Watters and most of the men he was tending to vanished instantly. "I could see the body parts on the trees," Manuel Orona recalled. "I shook myself off, and I got up. It was so quiet for about fifteen seconds, and then the screams. Mom, mom… my legs are gone!"[287] The bomb left a crater the size of a dump truck, with the blast extending past the casualty collection point, killing forty-two men and injuring another forty-five. Tom Remington, himself badly wounded, crawled over dead bodies to find a radio. When he finally got the headset up to his mouth, he yelled, "Stop those airplanes; they are killing us up here!"[288]

The night fell, only for the NVA to resume its attack on the American position. Men fought off attack after attack, some with their dead friends still lying beside them in their foxholes. Many of those who survived later spoke about the scary feeling of being alone, with the inevitability of death hanging over them. And the smell of death all around them. Nobody was cheering when the 4th Battalion finally reached their position in the early morning hours. Both groups silently nodded to each other, and then someone from a nearby foxhole asked for water. The Battle for Hill 875 had cost more than 100 American lives and wounded another 250, with 7 never found. The fight continued for another three days until the hill was finally in American hands. As was often the case, the NVA had slipped away across the border to safety in Cambodia. Within a week, the American forces would abandon the hillside.

Four days after the worst case of friendly fire of the entire conflict, on November 23, 1967, Thanksgiving Day, the replacement paratroopers and some of the original 173rd members found equipment that belonged to Father Watters. One of the men found the chalice and brought it over to the new chaplain, Reverend Roy Peters of California. Standing on Hill 875, Father Peters looked at the man who handed him the artifact and said, "If you want to talk about men—there was a real hero."[289]

# IN THE LAND OF A MILLION ELEPHANTS

The presentation was the first for President Richard Nixon, and he said it was his highest honor as the nation's executive. Three men stood at attention in the colorful East Room for a private ceremony. They represented nearly all the nation's regions, symbolizing the conflict's impact on all Americans. One young man was from California, one from Texas and the last in line from New Jersey. Sergeant Fred W. Zabitosky, known to his friends simply as "Zabs," stood quietly and waited his turn to receive the Medal of Honor. The Green Beret had survived the jungles of Vietnam; he lived where many had not. Unbeknownst to him, the ghosts of the conflict were only biding their time. Fred would pass away from cancer at fifty-three, tied to his exposure to Agent Orange during his time in Southeast Asia.[290]

Laos—landlocked between China in the north, Cambodia in the south, Thailand in the west and Vietnam in the east—played a pivotal yet often controversial and often forgotten role in the Vietnam War. By 1968, the United States' policy of attrition, based on the principle of inflicting massive losses on the enemy while minimizing its own, had cemented the nation in a stalemate. The issue lay with the fact that the Viet Cong and the North Vietnamese Army could control their losses by fighting the war at times and places of their own choosing and on ground favorable to them. If their losses reached unacceptable levels, the enemy melted away into the jungle or retreated into sanctuaries in North Vietnam, Cambodia or Laos.[291] At the same time, the United States, at least until the latter stages of the war, could not openly challenge this strategy without bringing about further repercussions from the antiwar movement at home. Because the Geneva Agreements that guided the French departure from Indochina the decade before banned the use of foreign troops in Cambodia and Laos, the U.S. relied on stealth when chasing the enemy into neutral albeit pro-Communist territory.[292] The nation's most significant weapon in this fight was the U.S. Army Special Forces, the Green Berets.

The only real home Fred William Zabitosky ever knew was the U.S. Army. Born in Trenton, New Jersey, in 1942 to a low-income family and minimal discipline, the young Fred was in trouble more often than he was not. His alcoholic father finally left the young man, his mother and his siblings when Fred was fifteen years old. Not seeing much choice, Zabitosky joined the army in 1959 to help supplement his mother's income. For the next few years, his brother, two sisters and mother would receive forty dollars from his sixty-dollar monthly pay.[293] With the escalation of the Vietnam War, Special Forces recruiters selected Staff Sergeant Zabitosky for advanced training in field survival, ambush techniques, small unit tactics and unconventional warfare.[294] The Green Beret training lasted seven months, and in 1965, Fred's unit, part of the 5th Special Forces Group, 1st Special Forces, was on the ground in Vietnam.

The New Jersey man rotated in and out of Vietnam for the next two years. The 5th Special Forces would become one of the most decorated units of the conflict, with sixteen Medals of Honor awarded to its members. Zabitosky's third tour in Southeast Asia and latest mission called for small teams, usually no more than ten to twelve men, to infiltrate Laos and Cambodia and monitor any movement on the Ho Chi Minh Trail. By December 1967, the staff sergeant had led twelve missions with mixed units of Americans and South Vietnamese into Laos, and while it was time for him to rotate out, the Tet Offensive of late January 1968 had changed all of that. On February 19, 1968, with the enemy's attacks still in full swing, Fred Zabitosky and his team received their newest orders to slip into Laos again and determine the enemy's troop concentration on the infamous hidden trail.

New Jersey governor Richard J. Hughes looks on as Sergeant First Class Fred Zabitosky signs the guest registrar prior to a hero's welcome by the legislature. *From the* Camden Courier Post, *1969.*

"I found myself somewhere in Laos walking on the Ho Chi Minh Trail, the most incredible thing I have ever seen," Jonathan Polansky recalled years later. "Underground hospitals of mammoth size, roads built with all that red dirt, chains of mountains with two-lane roads hacked out on the tops just going all the way down, big complexes of tree houses." It would be hard to deny that Laos was the enemy's safe haven despite being independent of the conflict and supposedly neutral. "We went into one cavern, and the tunnel alone was big enough for trucks to go through underground," Polansky added. "Thousands of rooms full of American equipment—boots, fatigues, cots, ponchos, helmets. They seemed to have more of our supplies than we had back at camp."[295]

Two Huey helicopters swooped down into the Laos jungle east of Attopeau. Zabs and his ten-men team jumped down, M16s at the ready, and fanned out as the helicopters rose above them. They were alone, yet it was nothing new and thus nothing to spend too much time thinking about. Major Michael Andrews, a platoon leader of a similar Combined Reconnaissance and Intelligence unit, attributed this attitude to the fact that "the men had been through [this] before." The men, he added, "were cohesive, knew their jobs rather well, and the opportunity of working together day in and day out and being independent and constantly training made the unit tactically proficient and unusually so." The Special Forces platoons, like the one Zabs was now leading onto the Ho Chi Minh Trail, also felt somewhat secure due to the speed with which they operated—in and out. "We were very small, and it was easier to keep on the move—we could move two or three days and not sleep in the same place or, during an operation, move quickly to be undetected," Andrews said. But this February 19, 1968, luck was not on their side.

Staff Sergeant Fred Zabitosky led his men away from the landing zone (LZ) and into the jungle when they suddenly came upon a previously unknown North Vietnamese Army complex with hundreds of bunkers and defensive positions and an overwhelming enemy force. The NVA discovered the Special Forces group almost instantly and opened fire. Zabs directed his troops to take up defensive positions as he lifted the semi-automatic rifle to his face and began picking off the advancing enemy soldiers. Directing fire as best he could, it soon became evident to the New Jersey man that the Vietnamese would flank his unit if they remained in the current position much longer. The sergeant yelled back at his men, ordering them to retreat toward the LZ. Remaining behind to cover the unit's withdrawal, the twenty-six-year-old man continued squeezing the trigger of his M16 and throwing grenades at the advancing NVA to buy himself time to reload his weapon.

When Zabs emerged from the thicket and into the open, the situation became more precarious because the called-in air support was still nowhere to be seen. The New Jerseyan directed the surviving members of his unit to take positions in a tight defensive perimeter and prepare their spare ammo and grenades for the oncoming onslaught. The small group of men could not know that they were holding on against a full assault by nearly four NVA companies.[296] When all hope was likely lost, two Huey carrier helicopters—nicknamed "slicks" since they did not contain mounted guns or rockets—appeared above them. The sergeant ordered his men to get inside the machines as bullets ricocheted off their metal, pinging inside the helicopter's hull before exiting the door openings on the other side. The enemy soldiers were almost directly in front of their position. Zabitosky waited for all men to board and, still firing his rifle, jumped into one of the Huey's just as it lifted off the ground. He was still firing the M16 while hanging out the door when the projectile hit the helicopter's tail.

The blast threw the New Jersey man out of the machine's door as the helicopter plummeted to the ground, crashing less than twenty feet from Zabitosky. A nearby NVA soldier running toward him sprang the sergeant out of his daze, making him launch toward his nearby rifle and take out the enemy. With the helicopter on fire and more fuel leaking out of the twisted metal, Zabitosky rushed toward the screams coming from inside. The wreckage was ablaze, and the heat unbearable as the New Jersey man lifted the severely wounded pilot out of the Huey and walked him a few yards away. By this time, the members of his unit in the second helicopter were firing from above, covering their commanding officer as best they could. Air support was only a minute away from their position, ready to blanket the area with napalm and conventional bombs. Zabitosky attempted to return to the flaming wreckage and rescue his patrol members, but the intense heat kept pushing him back.

The second helicopter landed, and Zabs had to know that it had become a now-or-never situation. Despite his serious burns, crushed ribs and broken back, the sergeant carried and dragged the unconscious pilot through a curtain of enemy fire to within ten feet of a hovering rescue helicopter. And then darkness. Sergeant Fred Zabitosky's determination was there—his body had just failed him. It robbed him of watching the air support arrive and drive back the enemy long enough for his men to drag him and the pilot up into the Huey and away to safety.

Zabitosky would return for his fourth tour of duty in Vietnam following the ceremony in which President Nixon awarded him the highest military honor. By the end of the conflict, he had received the Distinguished Service Cross, a Bronze Star, the Air Medal, the Combat Infantryman's Badge, two Army Commendation Medals and the Vietnamese Gallantry Cross with Bronze Star.[297] The long, costly and divisive conflict that pitted the United States and South Vietnam against North Vietnam took more than 3 million lives, including 58,000 Americans.[298] When news emerged that President Nixon had escalated the war from South Vietnam operations into Laos and Cambodia, violating international law, college campuses nationwide erupted in a new wave of protests. The shooting and killing of four students at Kent State University in Ohio in 1970 by National Guardsmen brought about the beginning of the end of U.S. involvement. In January 1973, the United States and North Vietnam concluded the final peace agreement, prompting the American military to withdraw that same year. The war between North Vietnam and its southern neighbor would continue until April 30, 1975, when Saigon fell to the Communists and was renamed Ho Chi Minh City.

# NOTES

*Preface*

1. Mikaelian, *Medal of Honor*, xvii.

*Introduction*

2. National Medal of Honor Museum, "The Highest and Most Prestigious Military Decoration," https://mohmuseum.org/the-medal/#:~:text=Of%20the%20 40%20million%20Americans,earned%20the%20Medal%20of%20Honor.
3. Mikaelian, *Medal of Honor*, xxv.
4. Ibid.
5. Ibid.
6. Collier, *Medal of Honor*, xx.
7. Official Site of the State of New Jersey, "World War II Memorial at Veterans Park," https://www.nj.gov/military/community/civic-engagement/war-memorials/wwii-memorial.shtml#:~:text=Over%20560%2C000%20New%20 Jerseyans%20served,support%20of%20the%20war%20effort.
8. Congressional Medal of Honor Society, "Nicholas Minue," https://www.cmohs.org/recipients/nicholas-minue.
9. Ibid.
10. "Lt. S.S. Coursen, Twice Decorated, Is Killed in Korea," *Madison (NJ) Eagle*, November 2, 1950, 1.
11. Congressional Medal of Honor Society, "Samuel Streit Coursen," https://www.cmohs.org/recipients/samuel-s-coursen.

12. Ibid., "Henry Svehla," https://www.cmohs.org/recipients/henry-svehla.

13. Quote Investigator, "All Wars Are Planned by Older Men," https://quoteinvestigator.com/2020/02/02/wars.

## Part I

14. Siegel, *Beneath the Starry Flag*, 62.

15. Ibid., 61.

16. Ibid., 63.

17. Ibid.

18. 1st Dragoon's Civil War Site, "The Biography of Corporal Charles Hopkins," https://dragoon1st.tripod.com/cw/files/hopkins1.html.

19. Ibid.

20. Ibid.

21. Hopkins, *Andersonville Diary and Memoirs of Charles Hopkins*, 193.

22. Ibid.

23. Ibid.

24. 1st Dragoon's Civil War Site, "The Biography of Corporal Charles Hopkins."

25. *American History*, 396.

26. Warner, *Generals in Gray*, 78.

27. Ibid.

28. Naval History and Heritage Command, "African American Sailors in the U.S. Navy," https://www.history.navy.mil/browse-by-topic/diversity/african-americans/chronology.html.

29. African American Veterans Monument, "The Stories of War: Spanish American War," https://aavmwny.org/war/spanish-american-war/#:~:text=When%20the%20United%20States%20declared,of%20Honor%20during%20the%20conflict.

30. Keenean, *Spanish-American and Philippine-American Wars*, 42.

31. Millett and Maslowski, *For the Common Defense*, 286.

32. Anthony Powell, "Black Participation in the Spanish American War," Spanish American War Centennial Website, https://www.spanamwar.com/AfroAmericans.htm.

33. "Expedition Landed: Captain Nunez Killed," *Rochester (NY) Democrat and Chronicle*, July 15, 1898, 2.

34. Ibid.

35. Cameron McR. Winslow, "Cable Cutting at Cienfuegos," May 1898, History of the Atlantic Cable & Undersea Communications, https://atlantic-cable.com/Article/1898CubaCablesCut/index.htm.

36. Ibid.

37. John Pelzer, "Spanish-American War: Raid on Cienfuegos," Historynet, https://www.historynet.com/spanish-american-war-raid-on-cienfuegos.

38. Winslow, "Cable Cutting at Cienfuegos."

39. Ibid.

40. Ibid.

41. Ibid.

42. Ibid.

## *Part II*

43. U.S. Army Center of Military History, "78th Infantry Division," https://history.army.mil/documents/eto-ob/78id-eto.htm.

44. Connors, *New Jersey and the Great War*, 111.

45. Ibid., 112.

46. Ibid., 113.

47. Military History Fandom, "John Otto Siegel," https://military-history.fandom.com/wiki/John_Otto_Siegel.

48. "A Hero Everyday," *Great Lakes Bulletin*, April, 22, 1919, 5.

49. Military History Fandom, "John Otto Siegel."

50. David T. Zabecki, "Hallowed Ground: Americans vs. Germans at Blanc Mont Ridge," Historynet, https://www.historynet.com/hallowed-ground-blanc-mont-ridge.

51. Eisenhower, *Yanks*, 137.

52. "Frank J. Bart, World War I Hero," *Herald News* (Passaic, NJ), April 1, 1961, 16.

53. Ibid.

54. Zabecki, "Hallowed Ground."

55. Mike Hanlon, "Forgotten Victory: Capturing Blanc Mont Ridge," World War I/The Great War, http://www.worldwar1.com/dbc/bm1.htm.

56. Ibid.

57. Ibid.

58. Zabecki, "Hallowed Ground."

59. Eisenhower, *Yanks*, 237.

60. Montgomery, *Story of Fourth Army*, 153.

61. Rod Leith, "WWI Committee Marks Centennial with Year-Long Remembrance," *South Bergenite* (Rutherford, NJ), January 8, 2015, B1.

62. Monash, *Australian Victories in France in 1918*, chapter 14.

63. Eisenhower, *Yanks*, 240.

64. American Battle Monuments Commission, "American Armies and Battlefields in Europe," 1939, 380, https://www.abmc.gov/sites/default/files/publications/Section6.pdf.

65. Ibid., 378.

66. Ibid., 379.

67. Ibid., 380.

68. Library of Congress, "Personal Narrative of Quincy Claude Ayers," https:// www.loc.gov/collections/veterans-history-project-collection/serving-our-voices/ world-war-i/world-war-i-rememebered-100-years-later/wwi-remembered-diaries-and-memoirs.

69. Thomason, *Fix Bayonets*, 13.

70. Ibid., 14.

71. Congressional Medal of Honor Society, "Alan Louis Eggers," https://www. cmohs.org/recipients/alan-l-eggers.

72. Thomason, *Fix Bayonets*, 81.

73. American Battle Monuments Commission, "American Armies and Battlefields in Europe," 380.

74. Kris Osborn, "Trio Earns Medals of Honor Saving Tank Soldiers in WWI," Center for Military Modernization, April 23, 2018, https://warriormaven.com/ history/trio-earns-medals-of-honor-saving-tank-soldiers-in-wwi.

75. Ibid.

76. Eric A. Dime, "United States War Hero Turned Out by the Krupps: How the Shy Little Dutch Sergeant Won that Dazzling Array of Medals," *Arkansas Gazette*, May 2, 1920, 13–15.

77. Ibid.

78. Ibid.

79. YouTube, "Ludovicus M.M. Van Iersel Interview," https://www.youtube.com/ watch?v=ciU6MBR9UNE.

80. Dime, "United States War Hero Turned Out by the Krupps."

81. Ibid.

82. Ibid.

83. Ibid.

84. YouTube, "Ludovicus M.M. Van Iersel Interview."

85. Ibid.

86. Dime, "United States War Hero Turned Out by the Krupps."

87. YouTube, "Ludovicus M.M. Van Iersel Interview."

88. Ibid.

89. Dime, "United States War Hero Turned Out by the Krupps."

## *Part III*

90. Bob Yehling and David Steele, "The Landing: From the Beaches of Iwo Jima to Suribachi's Peak," Defense Media Network, April 29, 2020, https://www.

defensemedianetwork.com/stories/the-landing-from-the-beaches-to-suribachis-peak-iwo-jima.

91. Ibid.

92. Bradley, *Flags of Our Fathers*, 64.

93. Bethanne Kelly Patrick, "Here's the Only Marine to Earn Both the Medal of Honor and Navy Cross during WWII," Military, https://www.military.com/history/marine-gunnery-sgt-john-basilone.html.

94. Ibid.

95. Bradley, *Flags of Our Fathers*, 161.

96. "Community's Grief Told Hero's Parents," *Plainfield (NJ) Courier News*, March 8, 1945, 1.

97. "Huge Crowd Greets Hero at Raritan," *Daily Home News* (New Brunswick, NJ), September 20, 1943, 1.

98. "Basilone Day Bond Sales Reach Total of 1,398,000," *Daily Home News* (New Brunswick, NJ), September 20, 1943, 5.

99. "Huge Crowd Greets Hero at Raritan," *Daily Home News* (New Brunswick, NJ), September 20, 1943, 5.

100. David A. Johnson, "The Battle for Henderson Field: The Harrowing Fight on Guadalcanal," Warfare History Network, https://warfarehistorynetwork.com/article/battle-for-henderson-field-the-harrowing-fight-on-guadalcanal.

101. Ibid.

102. *Time*, "Heroes: The Life and Death of Manila John" (March 19, 1945), https://content.time.com/time/subscriber/article/0,33009,797303-1,00.html.

103. Seth Paridon, "Life on Guadalcanal," National World War II Museum, October 2, 2017, https://www.nationalww2museum.org/war/articles/life-guadalcanal.

104. Ibid.

105. Johnson, "Battle for Henderson Field."

106. Ibid.

107. *Time*, "Heroes."

108. Johnson, "Battle for Henderson Field."

109. Patrick, "Here's the Only Marine."

110. *Time*, "Heroes."

111. Candy Hirschmann and Louis Scheinfeld, "Lindenwold Boy Saved from Fire by Marine Hero," *Courier Post* (Camden, NJ), April 11, 1963, 1.

112. Ibid., 3.

113. History, "Battle of Peleliu," August 21, 2018, https://www.history.com/topics/world-war-ii/battle-of-peleliu.

114. Spector, *Eagle Against the Sun*, 420–21.

115. Al Hemingway, "The Battle of Peleliu: Shocked Beyond Imagination," Warfare History Network, https://warfarehistorynetwork.com/the-battle-of-peleliu-shocked-beyond-imagination.

116. Ibid.

117. Spector, *Eagle Against the Sun*, 421.

118. Hemingway, "Battle of Peleliu."

119. Ibid.

120. "Carlton R. Rouh Dies, Medal of Honor Winner," *Courier Post* (Camden, NJ), December 9, 1977, 13.

121. Charles Humes, "What Do You Think?," *Courier Post* (Camden, NJ), October 21, 1948, 2.

122. Ibid.

123. Hemingway, "Battle of Peleliu."

124. Thomason, *Fix Bayonets*, 46.

125. "Pvt. Franklin E. Sigler, Little Falls Marine, to Get Medal of Honor at White House," *Paterson (NJ) Evening News*, October 1, 1945, 1, 12.

126. Ibid.

127. Bradley, *Flags of Our Fathers*, 242.

128. Ibid., 240.

129. Naval History and Heritage Command, "Battle of Iwo Jima," https://www.history.navy.mil/browse-by-topic/wars-conflicts-and-operations/world-war-ii/1945/battle-of-iwo-jima.html.

130. Marine Pass in Review, "Iwo Jima Eyewitness," February 1989, https://www.barracks.marines.mil/Portals/74/pass%20in%20review%20d/Feb%201989.pdf.

131. Ibid.

132. "Pvt. Franklin E. Sigler, Little Falls Marine."

133. Collier, *Medal of Honor*, 106.

134. Ibid.

135. Atkinson, *Guns at Last Light*, 209.

136. Ibid.

137. Ibid.

138. Ibid.

139. Ibid.

140. Ibid.

141. "Pvt. Franklin E. Sigler, Little Falls Marine."

142. Tucker-Jones, *Operation Dragoon*, 132.

143. Brian Swopes, "Tag Archives: 8th Air Force Mission No. 760: Medal of Honor, Brigadier General Frederick Walker Castle, Air Corps, United States Army," This Day in Aviation, https://www.thisdayinaviation.com/tag/8th-air-force-mission-no-760.

144. Ibid.

NOTES TO PAGES 96–106

145. Karen Abeyasekere, "'Bloody Hundredth' B-17 Pilot Shares WWII Experiences," U.S. Department of Defense, May 6, 2022, https://www.defense.gov/News/Feature-Stories/story/Article/3022302/bloody-hundredth-b-17-pilot-shares-wwii-experiences.

146. Swopes, "Tag Archives: 8th Air Force Mission No. 760."

147. Ibid.

148. American Air Museum in Britain, "Barbara Bartlett Remembers Robert W. Harriman," https://www.americanairmuseum.com/archive/person/robert-w-harriman.

149. Morgan Borin, Mountain Lakes Library director, interview by Peter Zablocki, February 10, 2023, Mountain Lakes, New Jersey.

150. "First Congressional Medal of Honor to a Camden Man," *Courier Post* (Camden, NJ), November 3, 1945, 3.

151. Dugard, "Taking Berlin," 210.

152. Ibid.

153. Ibid.

154. Steve McGraw, "Uncle Frank: Letter from Lori Head to the Nephew of Frank McGraw," http://www.stevemcgraw.com/dad/unclefrank/index.htm.

155. Ibid.

156. Ibid.

157. Ibid.

158. Frank Blazich, "The Quiet Hero from Camden: Francis X. McGraw," National Museum of American History, November 15, 2019, https://americanhistory.si.edu/blog/mcgraw.

159. Ibid.

160. Ibid.

161. U.S. Army Center of Military History, "Anzio 1944," https://history.army.mil/brochures/anzio/72-19.htm February 26, 2023.

162. Ibid.

163. "Awarded Bronze Star: Sgt. Anatole J. Simon, Jr.," *The Enterprise* (Ponchatoula, LA), March 16, 1945, 1.

164. "Pvt. John W. Dutko: He Died Killing Nazis," *New York Daily News*, October 9, 1944, 15.

165. Ibid.

166. Ibid.

167. Ibid.

168. Commander, Naval Surface Force Atlantic, "Battle of Anzio," https://www.surflant.usff.navy.mil.

169. "Pvt. John W. Dutko."

170. "Fourth Somerville Brother Slated to Don Uniform," *Courier News* (Plainfield, NJ), July 27, 1944, 10.

171. WWII Memorial Friends, "Battle of Nancy 75th Anniversary Commemoration at the WWII Memorial," https://wwiimemorialfriends. networkforgood.com/events/15300-battle-of-nancy-75th-anniversary-commemoration-at-the-wwii-memorial.

172. Nancy Stearns Theiss, "WWII Tank Commander Recounts Grim Details," *Courier Journal*, November 7, 2016, https://www.courier-journal.com/story/news/local/oldham/2016/11/07/wwii-tank-commander-recounts-grim-details/93419574.

173. Ibid.

174. World of Tanks Console, "Walter Stitt Interview," from WWII Tankers Share Their Stories, YouTube, https://www.youtube.com/watch?v=s_csRqwsgxM, 14:00.

175. Ibid., "Joe Caserta Interview," from WWII Tankers Share Their Stories, YouTube, https://www.youtube.com/watch?v=s_csRqwsgxM, 3:14.

176. Theiss, "WWII Tank Commander."

177. World of Tanks Console, "Walter Stitt Interview."

178. Ibid., "Joe Caserta Interview."

179. "Perth Amboy Man Given Son's Congressional Medal," *Asbury Park (NJ) Sunday Press*, April 22, 1945, 2.

180. WWII Memorial Friends, "Battle of Nancy 75th Anniversary Commemoration."

181. "Nation Honors Thorne at Ceremonies Today," *Asbury Park (NJ) Evening Press*, November 15, 1945, 6.

182. American Experience PBS, "Soldiers' Battlefield Accounts," https://www.pbs.org/wgbh/americanexperience/features/bulge-dispatches.

183. "Nation Honors Thorne at Ceremonies Today."

184. "Honor Cpl. Thorne at Ceremony Today," *Matawan (NJ) Journal*, November 15, 1945, 1.

185. Ibid.

186. Ibid.

187. Leckie, *Wars of America*, 816–17.

188. Maxim Chornyi, "Third Reich and Nazi Sites in Nuremberg," War Documentary: Travel Your Own History, June 28, 2019, https://war-documentary.info/nuremberg-reich-buildings.

189. History Place, "Triumph of the Will," https://www.historyplace.com/worldwar2/triumph/tr-will.htm.

190. Ibid.

191. Ibid.

192. Robert H. Jackson Center, "Cathedral in Ruins, Nuremberg Germany 1945–1946," June 29, 2015, https://www.roberthjackson.org/artifact/cathedral-in-ruins/#:~:text=Nuremberg%20was%20severely%20damaged%20in,killed%20and%20roughly%20100%2C000%20displaced.

193. Katie Lange, "Medal of Honor: Army 1st Lt. Francis Burke," U.S. Department of Defense, May 4, 2020, https://www.defense.gov/News/Feature-Stories/story/Article/2172846/medal-of-honor-monday-army-1st-lt-francis-burke.

194. Zita Ballinger Fletcher, "Breaking the City of Kings: The Battle for Nuremberg, 1945," Historynet, April 9, 2020, https://www.historynet.com/breaking-the-city-of-kings-the-battle-for-nuremberg-1945.

195. Ibid.

196. Ibid.

197. Ibid.

198. Lange, "Medal of Honor: Army 1st Lt. Francis Burke."

199. Ibid.

200. Congressional Medal of Honor Society, "Francis Xavier Burke," https://www.cmohs.org/recipients/francis-x-burke.

201. Fletcher, "Breaking the City of Kings."

202. Lange, "Medal of Honor: Army 1st Lt. Francis Burke."

203. Hastings, *Retribution*, 369.

204. O'Reilly and Dugard, *Killing the Rising Sun*, 99.

205. Hastings, *Retribution*, 369, 371.

206. Dower, *War without Mercy*, 45.

207. Real Time History, "Biggest U.S. Battle in the Pacific: Okinawa 1945," YouTube, https://www.youtube.com/watch?v=ha5WvjOF7Rc, 13:30.

208. Ibid., 11:30.

209. O'Reilly and Dugard, *Killing the Rising Sun*, 102.

210. Ibid.

211. "Medal of Honor Holder Gets County Court Job," *Herald News* (Passaic, NJ), June 28, 1946, 11.

212. Dower, *War without Mercy*, 61.

213. Real Time History, "Biggest U.S. Battle in the Pacific: Okinawa 1945," 13:58.

214. Pablo Villa, "This Month in NCO History: One-Man Charge at Ozato, Okinawa," Army University Press, https://www.armyupress.army.mil/Journals/NCO-Journal/Archives/2016/June/This-Month-in-NCO-History-June-1-1945-A-One-Man-Charge-at-Ozato-Okinawa.

215. Ibid.

216. The Conversation, "Battle of Okinawa's Legacy Lives on 70 Years Later as Locals Chafe Against Japanese Rule," April 1, 2015, https://theconversation.com/battle-of-okinawas-legacy-lives-on-70-years-later-as-locals-chafe-against-japanese-rule-us-arms-39357.

## *Part IV*

217. Newman Wright, "Hero Nervous as President Decorates Him," *Herald News* (Passaic-Clifton, NJ), November 25, 1952, 2.

218. Ibid.

219. Ibid.

220. National Medal of Honor Museum, "The Battle of the Chosin Reservoir and the Medal of Honor," June 23, 2022, https://mohmuseum.org/chosinreservoir.

221. Brady, *Coldest War*, 87.

222. Michael S. Lockett, "Remembering the Forgotten War: Chosin Veteran Recalls Korea," *Daily World*, November 10, 2022, https://www.thedailyworld.com/news/remembering-the-forgotten-war-chosin-veteran-recalls-korea.

223. National Medal of Honor Museum, "Battle of the Chosin Reservoir."

224. Brady, *Coldest War*, 221.

225. Lockett, "Remembering the Forgotten War."

226. Sam Roberts, "Hector A. Cafferata, 86, Dies; Given Medal of Honor for Korea Heroics," *New York Times*, April 14, 2016, https://www.nytimes.com/2016/04/15/us/hector-a-cafferata-a-medal-of-honor-recipient-dies-at-86.html.

227. Justo Bautista, "The Heroes Among Us," *Daily Record* (Morristown, NJ), November 7, 1976, B6.

228. Ibid.

229. Roberts, "Hector A. Cafferata."

230. Ibid.

231. Ned Forney, "The Battle of the Chosin Reservoir," October 17, 2018, Official Website of the United States Marine Corps, https://www.marfork.marines.mil/News/News-Article-Display/Article/1665198/the-battle-of-the-chosin-reservoir.

232. PBS, "American Experience: The Battle for Chosin, Chapter 1," November 1, 2016, retrieved March 8, 2023.

233. Ibid.

234. Katie Lange, "Medal of Honor Monday: Army Sgt. 1st Class Nelson Brittin," U.S. Department of Defense, March 7, 2022, https://www.defense.gov/News/Feature-Stories/story/Article/2952223/medal-of-honor-monday-army-sgt-1st-class-nelson-brittin.

235. Halberstam, *Coldest Winter*, 549.

236. Ibid.

237. "N.J. Hero's Mother to Receive Medal," *Plainfield (NJ) Courier News*, 1.

238. William Gallo, "How the Afghanistan Withdrawal Looks from South Korea, America's Other 'Forever War,'" VOA News, August 20, 2021, https://www.voanews.com/a/usa_how-afghanistan-withdrawal-looks-south-korea-americas-other-forever-war/6209777.html.

239. Bautista, "Heroes Among Us," B6.

240. Ibid.

241. Herring, *America's Longest War*, ix.

242. Caputo, *Rumor of War*, xiii.

243. Theodore Roosevelt, "Citizenship in a Republic," delivered at the Sorbonne, Paris, France, April 23, 1910, World Future Fund, https://www.worldfuturefund.org/Documents/maninarena.htm.

244. "250 Attend Hero's Rite," *The Record* (Hackensack, NJ), December 1, 1969, B-5.

245. Caputo, *Rumor of War*, xv.

246. "A Dead Hero Gets Our Highest Honor," *The Record* (Hackensack, NJ), November 2, 1969, 8-A.

247. Caputo, *Rumor of War*, xv.

248. Jack Hartzel, "Con Thien: The Hill of the Angels, Quang Tri Providence 1967," Vietnam Veterans Home Page, http://www.vietvet.org/jhconthn.htm.

249. Ibid.

250. Ibid.

251. Ibid.

252. "Medal of Honor Sought for Slain Marine Hero," *The Record* (Hackensack, NJ), November 10, 1967, 1.

253. Ibid.

254. Hartzel, "Con Thien."

255. "LBJ Honoring Hero, Cites Dissent," *The Record* (Hackensack, NJ), May 3, 1967, 18.

256. Santoli, *Everything We Had*, 63.

257. Ibid., 43.

258. Ibid.

259. Historynet, "Book Review—Snake's Daughter: The Roads In and Out of War (by Gail Hosking)," August 8, 2001, https://www.historynet.com/book-review-snakes-daughter-the-roads-in-and-out-of-war-by-gail-hosking-gilberg-vn.

260. Katie Lange, "Medal of Honor Monday: Army MSgt. Charles Hosking Jr.," U.S. Department of Defense, March 21, 2022, https://www.defense.gov/News/Feature-Stories/Story/Article/2969271/medal-of-honor-monday-army-msgt-charles-hosking-jr.

261. Jacobs, *If Not Now, When?*, 134–35.

262. "Fords Man a Hero," *Daily Home News* (New Brunswick, NJ), October 9, 1969, 1.

263. Jacobs, *If Not Now, When?*, 45.

264. Medal of Honor Book, "Jack Jacobs, Medal of Honor, Vietnam War: Interview," YouTube, https://www.youtube.com/watch?v=otM8AroOvEk, 1:40.

265. Santoli, *Everything We Had*, 94.

266. Herring, *America's Longest War*, 185.

267. Bill of Rights Institute, "Walter Cronkite Speaks Out Against Vietnam, February 27, 1968," https://billofrightsinstitute.org/activities/walter-cronkite-speaks-out-against-vietnam-february-27-1968.

268. Jacobs, *If Not Now, When?*, 8.

269. Medal of Honor Book, "Jack Jacobs," 5:38.

270. Ibid., 7:00.

271. Jacobs, *If Not Now, When?*, 133.

272. Ibid., 134.

273. Ibid., 133.

274. Ibid., 136.

275. Ibid.

276. History Channel, "Combat Zone: Hill 875," March, 5, 2007, YouTube, https://www.youtube.com/watch?v=auxBZNJt5CI, 32:00.

277. John Ismay, "The Secret History of a Vietnam War Airstrike Gone Terribly Wrong," *New York Times*, January 31, 2019, https://www.nytimes.com/2019/01/31/magazine/vietnam-war-airstrike-dak-to.html.

278. Dan Sheridan, "Grieving, Paramus Remembers the Hero Priest of Dak To," *The Record* (Hackensack, NJ), November 28, 1967, B-12.

279. Ibid.

280. Vietnam Veterans Memorial Fund, "Charles Watters," https://www.vvmf.org/stories/Charles-Watters-2.

281. History Channel, "Combat Zone: Hill 875."

282. Ibid.

283. Ibid.

284. Ibid., 28:00.

285. Ibid., 27:00.

286. Sheridan, "Grieving, Paramus Remembers."

287. History Channel, "Combat Zone: Hill 875," 32:00.

288. Ibid.

289. Sheridan, "Grieving, Paramus Remembers."

290. Ewing Township, New Jersey Official Website, "Biography of Fred Zabitosky," https://www.ewingnj.org/zabitosky-biography.

291. Herring, *America's Longest War*, 154.

292. Joseph Craig, "Green Berets Wage Secret War in Land of a Million Elephants," Association of the United States Army, November 29, 2018, https://www.ausa.org/articles/green-berets-wage-secret-war-%E2%80%98land-million-elephants%E2%80%99#:~:text=The%20U.S.%20Army%20Special%20Forces,next%20door%20in%20South%20Vietnam.

293. Kent DeLong, "History of the NCO SSG Fred W. Zabitosky," OCLC Inc., https://cgsc.contentdm.oclc.org/digital/api/collection/p15040coll2/id/5842/download.

294. Ibid.

295. Santoli, *Everything We Had*, 168.

296. "Nation's Top Honor to Jersey Soldier," *Daily Record* (Red Bank, NJ), March 10, 1969, 3.

297. Ibid.

298. History Channel, "Vietnam War," https://www.history.com/topics/vietnam-war/vietnam-war-history#kent-state-shooting.

# SELECTED BIBLIOGRAPHY

*American History.* Orlando, FL: Houghton Mifflin Harcourt Publishing Company, 2018.

Atkinson, Rick. *The Day of Battle: The War in Sicily and Italy, 1943–1944.* New York: Macmillan Publishers, 2008.

———. *The Guns at Last Light: The War in Western Europe, 1944–1945.* New York: Macmillan Publishers, 2014.

Bilby, Joseph G., and William C. Goble. *Remember You Are Jerseymen!: A Military History of New Jersey's Troops in the Civil War.* Charleston, SC: The History Press, 1998.

Bradley, James. *Flags of Our Fathers.* New York: Bantam Books, 64.

Brady, James. *The Coldest War: A Memoir of Korea.* New York: St. Martin's Press, 2007.

Caputo, Philip. *A Rumor of War.* New York: Henry Hold and Company, 2017.

Collier, Peter. *Medal of Honor, Revised & Updated Third Edition: Portraits of Valor Beyond the Call of Duty.* New York: Artisan, 2016.

Connors, Richard J. *New Jersey and the Great War.* Pittsburgh, PA: Dorrance Publishing Company, 2017.

Dower, John W. *War without Mercy: Race and Power in the Pacific War.* New York: Pantheon Books, 1986.

Dugard, Martin. *Taking Berlin: The Bloody Race to Defeat the Third Reich.* New York: Dutton Caliber, 2022.

Edelman, Bernard. *Dear America: Letters Home from Vietnam.* New York: W.W. Norton & Company, 2002.

Eisenhower, John S.D. *Yanks: The Epic Story of the American Army in World War I.* New York: Touchstone, 2001.

Foster, John Young. *New Jersey and the Rebellion: A History of the Services of the Troops and People of New Jersey in Aid of the Union Cause.* Trenton: State of New Jersey, 1868.

Halberstam, David. *The Coldest Winter: America and the Korean War.* New York: Hyperion, 2008.

Hastings, Max. *Retribution: The Battle for Japan, 1944–45.* New York: Vintage, 2009.

Herring, George C. *America's Longest War: The United States and Vietnam, 1950–1975.* New York: John Wiley & Sons, New York, 1979.

Hopkins, Charles. *The Andersonville Diary and Memoirs of Charles Hopkins.* Kearny, NJ: Belle Grove Publishing Company, 1988.

Jacobs, Colonel Jack, and Douglas Century. *If Not Now, When?: Duty and Sacrifice in America's Time of Need.* London, UK: Penguin, 2008.

Keenean, Jerry. *Spanish-American and Philippine-American Wars.* Santa Barbara, CA: ABC-Clio, 2001, 42.

Leckie, Robert. *The Wars of America.* New York: Harper and Row Publishers, 1981.

Lender, Mark Edward. *One State in Arms: A Short Military History of New Jersey.* Trenton: New Jersey Historical Society, 1991.

McCarthy, Tom. *The Greatest Medal of Honor Stories Ever Told.* Lanham, MD: Rowman & Littlefield, 2018.

McNally, Bernard. *Soldiers and Sailors of New Jersey in the Spanish-American War, Embracing a Chronological Account of the Army and Navy.* Classic Reprint. London, UK: Forgotten Books, 2018.

Mears, Dwight S. *The Medal of Honor: The Evolution of America's Highest Military Decoration.* Lawrence: University Press of Kansas, 2018.

Mikaelian, Allen. *Medal of Honor: Profiles of America's Military Heroes from the Civil War to the Present.* Rockland, MA: Wheeler Publishing Inc., 2002.

Millett, Allan R., and Peter Maslowski. *For the Common Defense: A Military History of the United States of America.* New York: Free Press, 1994.

Monash, John. *The Australian Victories in France in 1918.* London, UK: Hutchinson & Company, 1920.

Montgomery, Archibald. *The Story of Fourth Army in the Battles of the Hundred Days.* London, UK: Hodder and Stoughton, 1919.

Murphy, Edward F. *Vietnam Medal of Honor Heroes.* Exp. and rev. ed. New York: Presidio Press, 2010.

O'Reilly, Bill, and Martin Dugard. *Killing the Rising Sun: How America Vanquished World War II Japan.* New York: Henry Holt and Company, 2016.

Petriello, David. *Military History of New Jersey.* Charleston, SC: Arcadia Publishing, 2014.

Proser, Jim, and Jerry Cutter. *I'm Staying with My Boys: The Heroic Life of Sgt. John Basilone, USMC.* New York: Macmillan Publishers, 2010.

Robertson, James I., Jr. *The Civil War Letters of General Robert McAllister.* Baton Rouge: Louisiana State University Press, 1998.

Santoli, Al. *Everything We Had: An Oral History of the Vietnam War*. New York: Ballantine Books, 1985.

Siegel, Alan A. *Beneath the Starry Flag: New Jersey's Civil War Experience*. Piscataway, NJ: Rutgers University Press, 2001.

Sledge, Eugene Bondurant. *With the Old Breed*. New York: Random House, 2011.

Spector, Ronald H. *Eagle Against the Sun: The American War with Japan*. New York: Free Press, 2020.

Thomason, John William. *Fix Bayonets!* New York: C. Scribner, 1926.

Tuchman, Barbara W. *The Guns of August: The Outbreak of World War I*. Barbara W. Tuchman's Great War Series. New York: Random House, 2009.

Tucker-Jones, Anthony. *Operation Dragoon: The Liberation of Southern France 1944*. United Kingdom: Pen and Sword, 2010.

Warner, Ezra. *Generals in Gray: Lives of the Confederate Commanders*. Baton Rouge: Louisiana State University Press, 1959.

Willbanks, James H. *America's Heroes: Medal of Honor Recipients from the Civil War to Afghanistan*. Santa Barbara, CA: ABC-Clio, 2011.

# INDEX

# ABOUT THE AUTHOR

Peter Zablocki is a historian, educator and author of numerous books detailing New Jersey as well as American history. He is the recipient of the New Jersey Studies Academic Alliance Non-Fiction Popular Book of the Year Award and the Army Historical Foundation Distinguished Writing Award for Journals and Magazines. His articles often appear in various popular history publications, and his podcast, *History Teachers Talking*, is available on all popular streaming platforms. For more information about his books, podcast or any upcoming events, visit www.peterzablocki.com.